Antigone

ALSO BY ROBERT BAGG

Madonna of the Cello: Poems (Wesleyan University Press)

Euripides' Hippolytos (Oxford University Press)

The Scrawny Sonnets and Other Narratives
(Illinois University Press)

Euripides' The Bakkhai (University of Massachusetts Press)

Sophocles' Oedipus the King
(University of Massachusetts Press)

Body Blows: Poems New and Selected
(University of Massachusetts Press)

The Oedipus Plays of Sophocles with Notes and Introductions by Robert
and Mary Bagg (University of Massachusetts Press)

Niké and Other Poems (Azul Editions)

HORSEGOD: Collected Poems (iUniverse)

Euripides III: Hippolytos and Other Plays
(Oxford University Press)

The Tandem Ride and Other Excursions
(Spiritus Mundi Press)

The Complete Plays of Sophocles with James Scully
(Harper Perennial)

The Oedipus Cycle
(Harper Perennial)

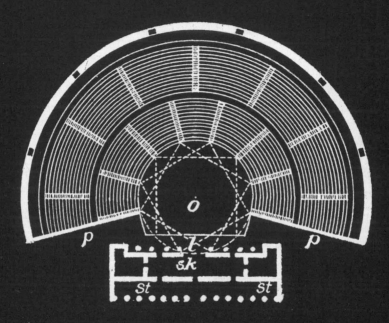

ANTIGONE

A New Translation by Robert Bagg

SOPHOCLES

HARPER ● PERENNIAL

NEW YORK ● LONDON ● TORONTO ● SYDNEY ● NEW DELHI ● AUCKLAND

HARPER ● PERENNIAL

For performance rights to *Antigone* contact The Strothman Agency, LLC, at 197 Eighth Street, Flagship Wharf – 611, Charlestown, MA 02129, or by email at info@strothmanagency.com.

HarperCollins books may be purchased for educational, business, or sales promotional use. For information, please e-mail the Special Markets Department at SPsales@harpercollins.com.

FIRST EDITION

Designed by Justin Dodd

Library of Congress Cataloging-in-Publication Data is available upon request.

ISBN 978-0-06-213212-3   /RRD

15 16 17 18   /RRD   16 15 14 13 12 11 10 9

For Barbara Smith, who directed the first performances
of my translation of Antigone *at the University of Utah's*
Greek Drama Festival in September 2001

CONTENTS

When Theater Was Life:
The World of Sophocles   xi

Antigone
    Introduction: "From What Kind of Parents
        Was I Born?"   1
    Play   11

Notes to the Play   89
Works Cited and Consulted   115
Acknowledgments   121
About the Translator   123

WHEN THEATER WAS LIFE: THE WORLD OF SOPHOCLES

I

Greek theater emerged from the same explosive creativity that propelled the institutions and ways of knowing of ancient Athens, through two and a half millennia, into our own era. These ranged from the concept and practice of democracy, to an aggressive use of logic with few holds barred, to a philosophy singing not of gods and heroes but of what exists, where it came from, and why. Athenians distinguished history from myth, acutely observed the human form, and reconceived medicine from a set of beliefs and untheorized practices into a science.

Playwrights, whose work was presented to audiences of thousands, effectively took center stage as critics and interpreters of their own culture. Athenian drama had one major showing each year at the nine-day Festival of Dionysos. It was rigorously vetted. Eight dramatists (three tragedians, five comic playwrights), chosen in open competition, were "granted choruses," a down-to-earth term meaning that the city financed production of their plays. For the Athenians theater was as central to civic life as the assembly, law courts, temples, and agora.

Historians summing up Athens' cultural importance have tended to emphasize its glories, attending less to the brutal institutions and policies that underwrote the city's wealth and dominance: its slaves, for instance, who worked the mines that enriched the communal treasury; or its policy of executing the men and enslaving the women and children of enemy cities that refused to surrender on demand. During its long war with Sparta, Athens' raw and unbridled democracy became increasingly reckless, cruel, and eventually self-defeating. Outside the assembly's daily debates on war, peace, and myriad other issues, Athenian citizens, most notably the indefatigable Socrates, waged ongoing critiques of the city's actions and principles. Playwrights, whom the Athenians called *didaskaloi* (educators), were expected to enlighten audiences about themselves, both individually and collectively. As evidenced by the thirty-three plays that survive, these works presented a huge audience annually with conflicts and dilemmas of the most extreme sort.

To some extent all Sophocles' plays engage personal, social, and political crises and confrontations—not just those preserved in heroic legend but those taking place in his immediate world. Other Athenian intellectuals, including Thucydides, Aeschylus, Euripides, Plato, and Aristophanes, were part of that open-ended discussion in which everything was subject to question, including the viability of the city and its democracy (which was twice voted temporarily out of existence).

II

To this day virtually every Athenian theatrical innovation—from paraphernalia such as scenery, costumes, and masks to the architecture of stage and seating and, not least, to the use of drama as a powerful means of cultural and political commentary—remains in use. We thus inherit from Athens the vital *potential* for drama to engage our realities and to support or critique prevailing orthodoxies.

The myths that engaged Sophocles' audience originated in Homer's epics of the Trojan War and its aftermath. Yet Homer's world was tribal. That of the Greek tragedians was not, or only nominally so. With few exceptions (e.g., Aeschylus' *The Persians*), those playwrights were writing *through* the Homeric world to address, and deal with, the *polis* world they themselves were living in. Sophocles was appropriating stories and situations from these epics, which were central to the mythos of Athenian culture, and re-visioning them into dramatic *agons* (contests) relevant to the tumultuous, often vicious politics of Greek life in the fifth century BCE. Today some of Sophocles' concerns, and the way he approached them, correspond at their deepest levels to events and patterns of thought and conduct that trouble our own time. For example, "[Sophocles'] was an age when war was endemic. And Athens in the late fifth century BC appeared to have a heightened taste for conflict. One year of two in the Democratic Assembly, Athenian citizens voted in favor of military aggression" (Hughes, 138).

Each generation interprets and translates these plays in keeping with the style and idiom it believes best suited for tragedy.

Inevitably even the most skilled at preserving the original's essentials, while attuning its voice to the present, will eventually seem the relic of a bygone age. We have assumed that a contemporary translation should attempt to convey not only what the original seems to have been communicating, but *how* it communicated—not in its saying, only, but in its *doing*. It cannot be said too often: these plays were social and historical *events* witnessed by thousands in a context and setting infused with religious ritual and civic protocol. They were not transitory, one-off entertainments but were preserved, memorized, and invoked. Respecting this basic circumstance will not guarantee a successful translation, but it is a precondition for giving these works breathing room in which their strangeness, their rootedness in distinct historical moments, can flourish. As with life itself, they were not made of words alone.

Athenian playwrights relied on a settled progression of scene types: usually a prologue followed by conversations or exchanges in which situations and attitudes are introduced, then a series of confrontations that feature cut-and-thrust dialogue interrupted by messenger narratives, communal songs of exultation or grieving, and less emotionally saturated, or 'objective,' choral odes that respond to or glance off the action. Audiences expected chorus members to be capable of conveying the extraordinary range of expressive modes, from the pithy to the operatic, that Sophocles had at his disposal. To translate this we have needed the resources not only of idiomatic English but also of rhetorical gravitas and, on occasion, colloquial English. Which is why we have adopted, regarding vocabulary and 'levels of speech,' a wide and varied palette. When Philoktetes

exclaims, "You said it, boy," that saying corresponds in charac-
ter to the colloquial Greek expression. On the other hand Aias's
"Long rolling waves of time . . ." is as elevated, without being
pompous, as anything can be.

Unfortunately we've been taught, and have learned to live
with, washed-out stereotypes of the life and art of 'classical'
times—just as we have come to associate Greek sculpture with
the color of its underlying material, usually white marble. The
classical historian Bettany Hughes writes in *The Hemlock Cup*
(81) that temples and monuments were painted or stained in
"Technicolor" to be seen under the bright Attic sun. The stat-
ues' eyes were not blanks gazing off into space. They had color:
a *look*. To restore their flesh tones, their eye color, and the
bright hues of their cloaks would seem a desecration. We should
understand that this is so—even as we recognize that, for us,
there is no going back. We've been conditioned to preserve not
the reality of ancient Greek sculpture in its robust cultural am-
bience and physical setting, but our own fixed conception of it
as colorless and sedate—a perception created, ironically, by the
weathering and ravages of centuries. No one can change that.
Still, as translators we have a responsibility not to reissue a ste-
reotype of classical Greek culture but rather to recoup, to the
extent possible, the vitality of its once living reality.

Regarding its highly inflected language, so different from our
more context-driven modern English, we recognize that locu-
tions sounding contorted, coy, recondite, or annoyingly round-
about were a feature of ordinary Greek and were intensified in
theatrical discourse. Highly wrought, larger-than-life expres-
sions, delivered without artificial amplification to an audience

of thousands, did not jar when resonating in the vast Theater of
Dionysos, but may to our own Anglophone ears when delivered
from our more intimate stages and screens, or read in our books
and electronic tablets. Accordingly, where appropriate, and es-
pecially in rapid exchanges, we have our characters speak more
straightforwardly—as happens in Greek stichomythia, when
characters argue back and forth in alternating lines (or 'rows')
of verse, usually linked by a word they hold in common. Here,
for example, is a snippet from *Aias* (1305–1309)[1] that pivots on
"right," "killer," "dead" and "god(s)":

TEUKROS   A righteous cause is my courage.
MENELAOS What? It's right to defend my killer?
TEUKROS   Your killer!? You're dead? And still alive?
MENELAOS A god saved me. But he *wanted* me dead.
TEUKROS   If the gods saved you, why disrespect them?

There are no rules for determining when a more-literal or
less-literal approach is appropriate. Historical and dramatic
context have to be taken into account. The objective is not
only to render the textual meaning (which is ordinarily more
on the phrase-by-phrase than the word-by-word level) but also
to communicate the feel and impact embedded in that mean-
ing. Dictionaries are indispensable for translators, but they are
not sufficient. The meanings of words are immeasurably more
nuanced and wide-ranging in life than they can ever be in a
lexicon. As in life, where most 'sayings' cannot be fully grasped
apart from their timing and their place in both personal and
social contexts, so in theater: dramatic context must take words

up and finish them off. In *Aias*, Teukros, the out-of-wedlock half brother of Aias, and Menelaos, co-commander of the Greek forces, are trading insults. When Menelaos says, "The archer, far from blood dust, thinks he's something," Teukros quietly rejoins, "I'm very good at what I do" (1300–1301).

Understanding the exchange between the two men requires that the reader or audience recognize the 'class' implications of archery. Socially and militarily, archers rank low in the pecking order. They stand to the rear of the battle formation. Archers are archers usually because they can't afford the armor one needs to be a hoplite, a frontline fighter. The point is that Teukros refuses to accept 'his place' in the social and military order. For a Greek audience, the sheer fact of standing his ground against a commander had to have been audacious. But that is not how it automatically registers in most modern word-by-word translations, which tend to make Teukros sound defensive (a trait wholly out of his character in this play). Examples: (a) "Even so, 'tis no sordid craft that I possess," (b) "I'm not the master of a menial skill," (c) "My archery is no contemptible science," (d) "The art I practice is no mean one." These translations are technically accurate. They're scrupulous in reproducing the Greek construction whereby, in an idiomatic context, a negative may register as an assertion—or even, framed as a negative future question, become a command. But tonally, in modern English idiom, Teukros' negation undercuts his assertion (the 'I'm not . . . but even so' formula). To our ears it admits weakness or defensiveness. "I'm very good at what I do," however, is a barely veiled threat. The dramatic arc of the encounter, which confirms that Teukros will not back down for anything or anyone, not even a commander of the Greek army, substantiates that Sophocles meant it to be heard as such.

Hearing the line in context we realize instantly not only what the words are saying but, more pointedly and feelingly, what they're doing. His words are not just 'about' something. They are an act in themselves—not, as in the more literal translations, a duress-driven apologia. Translation must thus respond to an individual character's ever-changing demeanor and circumstance. The speaker's state of mind should show through his or her words, just as in life. Idiomatic or colloquial expressions fit many situations better—especially those that have a more finely tuned emotional economy—than phrases that, if uninhabited, hollowed out, or just plain buttoned-up, sound evasive or euphemistic. Many of the speeches Sophocles gives his characters are as abrupt and common as he might himself have spoken to his fellow Athenians in the assembly, in the agora, to his troops, his actors, or his family.

At times we have chosen a more literal translation in passages where scholars have opted for a seemingly more accessible modern phrase. At the climactic moment in *Oedipus the King*, when Oedipus realizes he has killed his father and fathered children with his mother, he says in a modern prose version by Hugh Lloyd-Jones: "Oh, oh! All is now clear. O light, may I now look on you for the last time, I who am revealed as cursed in my birth, cursed in my marriage, cursed in my killing!" (Greek 1182–1885). When Lloyd-Jones uses and repeats the word "cursed," he is compressing a longer Greek phrase meaning "being shown to have done what must not be done." This compression shifts the emphasis from his unsuspecting human

actions toward the realm of the god who acted to "curse" him.
The following lines keep the original grammatical construction:

> All! All! It has all happened!
> It was all true. O light! Let this
> be the last time I look on you.
> You see now who I am—
> the child who must not be born!
> I loved where I must not love!
> I killed where I must not kill! (1336–1342)

Here Oedipus names the three acts of interfamilial trans-
gression that it was both his good and his ill fortune to have
survived, participated in, and inflicted—birth, sexual love, and
murder in self-defense—focusing not only on the curse each act
has become but now realizing the full and horrific consequence
of each action that was, as it happened, unknowable. Register-
ing the shudder rushing through him, Oedipus's exclamations
convey the shock of his realization: *I did these things without
feeling their horror as I do now.*

Finally, translations tend to be more or less effective depend-
ing on their ability to convey the emotional and physiological
reactions that will give a reader or an audience a kinesthetic re-
lationship to the dramatic moment, whether realized as text or
performance. This is a precondition for maintaining the tactil-
ity that characterizes any living language. Dante wrote that the
spirit of poetry abounds "in the tangled constructions and de-
fective pronunciations" of vernacular speech where language is
renewed and transformed. We have not attempted that—these

are translations, not new works—but we have striven for a language that is spontaneous and generative as opposed to one that is studied and bodiless. We have also worked to preserve the root meaning of Sophocles' Greek, especially his always illuminating metaphors.

III

Sophocles reveals several recurrent attitudes in his plays—sympathy for fate's victims, hostility toward leaders who abuse their power, skepticism toward self-indulgent 'heroes,' disillusionment with war and revenge—that are both personal and politically significant. All his plays to a greater or lesser degree focus on outcasts from their communities. Historically, those who transgress a community's values have either been physically exiled or stigmatized by sanctions and/or shunning. To keep a polity from breaking apart, everyone, regardless of social standing, must abide by certain enforceable communal expectations. Athens in the fifth century BCE practiced political ostracism, a procedure incorporated in its laws. By voting to ostracize a citizen, Athens withdrew its protection and civic benefits—sometimes to punish an offender, but also as a kind of referee's move, expelling a divisive public figure from the city (and from his antagonists) so as to promote a ten-year period of relative peace.

In earlier eras Greek cities also cast out those who committed sacrilege. Murderers of kin, for instance, or blasphemers of a god—in myth and in real life—were banished from Greek cities until the 'unclean' individual 'purged' his crime according to current religious custom. The imperative to banish a kin violator runs so deep that Oedipus, after discovering he has committed patricide and incest, passes judgment on himself and demands to live in exile. In *Oedipus at Kolonos*, he and Antigone have been exiled from Thebes against their will. In the non-Oedipus plays the title characters Philoktetes, Elektra, and Aias, as well as Herakles in *Women of Trakhis*, are not outcasts in the traditional sense, though all have actively or involuntarily offended their social units in some way. They may or may not be typical tragic characters; nonetheless none 'fit' the world they're given to live in. In these translations we've incorporated awareness of social dimensions in the original texts, which, as they involve exercises of power, are no less political than social.

In each of the four non-Oedipus plays, a lethal confrontation or conflict 'crazes' the surface coherence of a society (presumed to be Athenian society, either in itself or as mediated through a military context), thus revealing and heightening its internal contradictions.

In *Women of Trakhis* the revered hero Herakles, when he tries to impose a young concubine on his wife Deianeira, provokes her to desperate measures that unwittingly cause him horrific pain, whereupon he exposes his savage and egomaniacal nature, lashing out at everyone around him, exercising a hero's prerogatives so savagely that he darkens his own reputation and drives his wife to suicide and his son to bitter resentment.

Elektra exposes the dehumanizing cost of taking revenge, by revealing the neurotic, materialistic, and cold-blooded character of the avengers. In *Aias*, when the Greek Army's most powerful soldier tries to assassinate his commanders, whose authority rests on dubious grounds, he exposes not only them but his own growing obsolescence in a prolonged war that has more need of strategic acumen, as exemplified by Odysseus, than brute force. In *Philoktetes* the title character, abandoned on a deserted island because of a stinking wound his fellow warriors can't live with, is recalled to active service with the promise of a cure and rehabilitation. The army needs him and his bow to win the war. It is a call he resists, until the god Herakles negotiates a resolution—not in the name of justice, but because Philoktetes' compliance is culturally mandated. As in *Aias*, the object is to maintain the integrity and thus the survival of the society itself. The greatest threat is not an individual's death, which here is not the preeminent concern, but the disintegration of a society.

In our own time aspects of *Aias* and *Philoktetes* have been used for purposes that Sophocles, who was the sponsor in Athens of a healing cult, might have appreciated. Both heroes, but especially Aias, have been appropriated as exemplars of post-traumatic stress disorder, in particular as suffered by soldiers in and out of a war zone. Excerpts from these two plays have been performed around the United States for veterans, soldiers on active duty, their families, and concerned others. Ultimately, however, Sophocles is intent on engaging and resolving internal contradictions that threaten the historical continuity, the very future, of the Athenian city-state. He invokes the class contradictions Athens was experiencing by applying them to the mythical/historical eras from which he draws his plots.

Modern-day relevancies implicit in Sophocles' plays will come sharply into focus or recede from view depending on time and circumstance. The constant factors in these plays will always be their consummate poetry, dramatic propulsion, and the intensity with which they illuminate human motivation and morality. Scholars have also identified allusions in his plays to events in Athenian history. The plague in *Oedipus the King* is described in detail so vivid it dovetails in many respects with Thucydides' more clinical account of the plague that killed one-third to one-half of Athens' population beginning in 429 BCE. Kreon, Antigone's antagonist, displays the imperviousness to rational advice and lack of foresight exhibited by the politicians of Sophocles' era, whose follies Thucydides narrates, and which Sophocles himself was called in to help repair—specifically by taking a democracy that in a fit of imperial overreach suffered, in 413, a catastrophic defeat on the shores of Sicily, and replacing it with a revanchist oligarchy. When Pisander, one of the newly empowered oligarchs, asked Sophocles if he was one of the councilors who had approved the replacement of the democratic assembly by what was, in effect, a junta of four hundred, Sophocles admitted that he had. "Why?" asked Pisander. "Did you not think this a terrible decision?" Sophocles agreed it was. "So weren't you doing something terrible?" "That's right. There was no better alternative." (Aristotle, Rh. 1419a). The lesson? When life, more brutally than drama, delivers its irreversible calamities and judgments, it forces a polity, most movingly, to an utterly unanticipated, wholly 'other' moral and spiritual level.

In *Oedipus at Kolonos* Sophocles alludes to his city's decline when he celebrates a self-confident Athens that no longer existed when Sophocles wrote that play. He gives us Theseus, a throwback to the type of thoughtful, decisive, all-around leader Athens lacked as it pursued policies that left it impoverished and defenseless—this under the delusion that its only enemies were Spartans and Sparta's allies.

IV

Archaeologists have identified scores of local theaters all over the Greek world—stone semicircles, some in cities and at religious destinations, others in rural villages. Within many of these structures both ancient and modern plays are still staged. Hillsides whose slopes were wide and gentle enough to seat a crowd made perfect settings for dramatic encounters and were the earliest theaters. Ancient roads that widened below a gentle hillside, or level ground at a hill's base, provided suitable performance spaces. Such sites, along with every city's agora and a temple dedicated to Dionysos or another god, were the main arenas of community activity. Stone tablets along roads leading to theaters commemorated local victors: athletes, actors, playwrights, singers, and the winning plays' producers. Theaters, in every sense, were open to all the crosscurrents of civic and domestic life.

The components of the earliest theaters reflect their rural origins and were later incorporated into urban settings. *Theatron*, the root of our word "theater," translates as "viewing place" and designated the curved and banked seating area. *Orchestra* was literally "the place for dancing." The costumed actors emerged from and retired to the *skenê*, a word that originally meant, and literally was in the rural theaters, a tent. As theaters evolved to become more permanent structures, the *skenê* developed as well into a "stage building" whose painted facade changed, like a mask, with the characters' various habitats. Depending on the drama, the *skenê* could assume the appearance of a king's grand palace, the Kyklops' cave, a temple to a god, or (reverting to its original material form) an army commander's tent.

Greek drama itself originated in two earlier traditions, one rural, one civic. Choral singing of hymns to honor Dionysos or other gods and heroes, which had begun in the countryside, evolved into the structured choral ode. The costumes and the dancing of choral singers, often accompanied by a reed instrument, are depicted on sixth-century vases that predate the plays staged in the Athenian theater. The highly confrontational nature of every play suggests how early choral odes and dialogues came into being in concert with a fundamental aspect of democratic governance: public and spirited debate. Two or more characters facing off in front of an audience was a situation at the heart of both drama and democratic politics.

Debate, the democratic Athenian art practiced and perfected by politicians, litigators, and thespians—relished and judged by voters, juries, and audiences—flourished in theatrical venues and permeated daily Athenian life. Thucydides used it to narrate his history of the war between Athens and Sparta. He recalled scores of lengthy debates that laid out the motives of politicians, generals, and diplomats as each argued his case for a particular policy or a strategy. Plato, recognizing the open-ended, exploratory power of spirited dialogue, wrote his philosophy entirely in dramatic form.

The Greeks were addicted to contests and turned virtually every chance for determining a winner into a formal competition. The Great Dionysia for playwrights and choral singers and the Olympics for athletes are only the most famous and familiar. The verbal *agon* remains to this day a powerful medium for testing and judging issues. And character, as in the debate between Teukros and Menelaos, may be laid bare. But there is no guarantee. Persuasiveness can be, and frequently is, manipulative (e.g., many of the sophists evolved into hired rhetorical guns, as distinguished from the truth-seeking, pre-Socratic philosophers). Sophocles may well have had the sophists' amorality in mind when he had Odysseus persuade Neoptomolos that betraying Philoktetes would be a patriotic act and bring the young man fame.

Though they were part of a high-stakes competition, the plays performed at the Dionysia were part of a religious ceremony whose chief purpose was to honor theater's patron god, Dionysos. The god's worshippers believed that Dionysos' powers and rituals transformed the ways in which they experienced and dealt with their world—from their enthralled response to theatrical illusion and disguise to the exhilaration, liberation, and violence induced by wine. Yet the festival also aired, or licensed, civic issues that might otherwise have had no truly public, *polis*-wide expression. The playwrights wrote as *politai*, civic poets, as distinguished from those who focused on personal lyrics and shorter choral works. Though *Aias* and *Philoktetes* are set in a military milieu, the issues they engage are essentially civil and political. Neither *Aias* nor *Philoktetes* is concerned with the 'enemy of record,' Troy, but rather with Greek-on-Greek conflict. With civil disruption, and worse. In fact one need look no further than the play venue itself for confirmation of the interpenetration of the civic with the military—a concern bordering on preoccupation—when, every year, the orphans of warriors killed in battle were given new hoplite armor and a place of honor at the Festival of Dionysos.

Communal cohesiveness and the historical continuity of the polity are most tellingly threatened from within: in *Aias* by the individualistic imbalance and arrogance of Aias, whose warrior qualities and strengths are also his weakness—they lead him to destroy the war spoil that is the common property of the entire Greek army—and in *Philoktetes* by the understandable and just, yet inordinately unyielding, self-preoccupation of Philoktetes himself. In both cases the fundamental, encompassing question is this: With what understandings, what basic values, is the commonality of the *polis* to be recovered and rededicated in an era in which civic cohesiveness is under the extreme pressure of a war Athens is losing (especially at the time *Philoktetes* was produced) and, further, the simmering stasis of unresolved class or caste interests? In sharply different ways, all three plays of the Oedipus cycle, as well as *Aias* and *Elektra*, cast doubt on the legitimacy of usurped, authoritarian, or publicly disapproved leadership.

Given the historical and political dynamism of these great, instructive works, we've aimed to translate and communicate their challenge to Athenian values for a contemporary audience whose own values are no less under duress.

V

The Great Dionysia was the central and most widely attended event of the political year, scheduled after winter storms had abated so that foreign visitors could come and bear witness to Athens' wealth, civic pride, imperial power, and artistic imagination. For eight or nine days each spring, during the heyday of Greek theater in the fifth century BCE, Athenians flocked to the temple grounds sacred to Dionysos on the southern slope of the Acropolis. After dark on the first day, a parade of young men hefted a giant phallic icon of the god from the temple and into the nearby theater. As the icon had been festooned with garlands of ivy and a mask of the god's leering face, their raucous procession initiated a dramatic festival called the City Dionysia, a name that differentiated it from the festival's ancient rural origins in Dionysian myth and cult celebrations of the god. As the festival gained importance in the sixth century BCE, most likely through the policies of Pisistratus, it was also known as the Great Dionysia.

Pisistratus, an Athenian tyrant in power off and on beginning in 561 BCE and continuously from 546 to 527, had good reason for adapting the Rural Dionysia as Athens' Great Dionysia: "Dionysos was a god for the 'whole' of democratic Athens" (Hughes, 213). Everyone, regardless of political faction or social standing, could relate to the boisterous communal activities of the festival honoring Dionysos: feasting, wine drinking, dancing, singing, romping through the countryside, and performing or witnessing dithyrambs and more elaborate dramatic works. The Great Dionysia thus served to keep in check, if not transcend, internal factionalizing by giving all citizens a 'natural' stake in Athens—Athens not simply as a place but as a venerable polity with ancient cultural roots. To this end Pisistratus had imported from Eleutherai an ancient phallic representation of Dionysos, one that took several men to carry.

Lodged as it was in a temple on the outskirts of Athens, this bigger-than-life icon gave the relatively new, citified cult the sanctified air of hoary antiquity (Csapo and Slater, 103–104). Thus validated culturally, the Great Dionysia was secured as a host to reassert, and annually rededicate, Athens as a democratic polity. As Bettany Hughes notes in *The Hemlock Cup*, "to call Greek drama an 'art-form' is somewhat anachronistic. The Greeks (unlike many modern-day bureaucrats) didn't distinguish drama as 'art'—something separate from 'society,' 'politics,' [or] 'life.' Theater was fundamental to democratic Athenian business. . . . [In] the fifth century this was the place where Athenian democrats came to understand the very world they lived in" (Hughes, 213).

The occasion offered Athens the chance to display treasure exacted from subjugated 'allies' (or tributes others willingly brought to the stage) and to award gold crowns to citizens whose achievements Athens' leaders wished to honor. Theater attendance itself was closely linked to citizenship; local town councils issued free festival passes to citizens in good standing. The ten generals elected yearly to conduct Athens' military campaigns poured libations to Dionysos. The theater's bowl seethed with a heady, sometimes unruly brew of military, political, and religious energy.

Performances began at dawn and lasted well into the

afternoon. The 14,000 or more Athenians present watched in god knows what state of anticipation or anxiety. Whatever else it did to entertain, move, and awe, Athenian tragedy consistently exposed human vulnerability to the gods' malice and favoritism. Because the gods were potent realities to Athenian audiences, they craved and expected an overwhelming emotional, physically distressing experience. That expectation distinguishes the greater intensity with which Athenians responded to plays from our own less challenging, more routine and frequent encounters with drama. Athenians wept while watching deities punish the innocent or unlucky, a reaction that distressed Plato. In his *Republic*, rather than question the motives or morality of the allpowerful Olympian gods for causing mortals grief, he blamed the poets and playwrights for their unwarranted wringing of the audience's emotions. He held that the gods had no responsibility for human suffering. True to form, Plato banned both poets and playwrights from his ideal city.

Modern audiences would be thoroughly at home with other, more cinematic stage effects. The sights and sounds tragedy delivered in the Theater of Dionysos were often spectacular. Aristotle, who witnessed a lifetime of productions in the fourth century—well after Sophocles' own lifetime, when the plays were performed in the heat of their historical moment—identified "spectacle," or *opsis*, as one of the basic (though to him suspect) elements of tragic theater. Under the influence of Aristotle, who preferred the study to the stage, and who therefore emphasized the poetry rather than the production of works, ancient commentators tended to consider "the visual aspects of drama [as] both vulgar and archaic" (Csapo and Slater, 257).

Nonetheless, visual and aural aspects there were: oboe music; dancing and the singing of set-piece odes by a chorus; masks that transformed the same male actor, for instance, into a swarthy-faced young hero, a dignified matron, Argos with a hundred eyes, or the Kyklops with only one. The theater featured painted scenery and large-scale constructions engineered with sliding platforms and towering cranes. It's hardly surprising that Greek tragedy has been considered a forerunner of Italian opera.

Judges awarding prizes at the Great Dionysia were chosen by lot from a list supplied by the council—one judge from each of Athens' ten tribes. Critical acumen was not required to get one's name on the list, but the *choregoi* (the producers and financial sponsors of the plays) were present when the jury was assembled and probably had a hand in its selection. At the conclusion of the festival the ten selected judges, each having sworn that he hadn't been bribed or unduly influenced, would inscribe on a tablet the names of the three competing playwrights in descending order of merit. The rest of the process depended on chance. The ten judges placed their ballots in a large urn. The presiding official drew five at random, counted up the weighted vote totals, and declared the winner.

VI

When Sophocles was a boy, masters trained him to excel in music, dance, and wrestling. He won crowns competing against his age-mates in all three disciplines. Tradition has it that he first appeared in Athenian national life at age fifteen, dancing naked (according to one source) and leading other boy dancers in a hymn of gratitude to celebrate Athens' defeat of the Persian fleet in the straits of Salamis.

Sophocles' father, Sophroniscus, manufactured weapons and armor (probably in a factory operated by slaves), and his mother, Phaenarete, was a midwife. The family lived in Kolonos, a rural suburb just north of Athens. Although his parents were not aristocrats, as most other playwrights' were, they surely had money and owned property; thus their status did not hamper their son's career prospects. Sophocles' talents as a dramatist, so formidable and so precociously developed, won him early fame. As an actor he triumphed in his own now-lost play, *Nausicaä*, in the role of the eponymous young princess who discovers the nearly naked Odysseus washed up on the beach while playing ball with her girlfriends.

During Sophocles' sixty-five-year career as a *didaskalos* he wrote and directed more than 120 plays and was awarded first prize at least eighteen times. No record exists of his placing lower than second. Of the seven entire works of his that survive, along with a substantial fragment of a satyr play, *The Trackers*, only two very late plays can be given exact production dates: *Philoktetes* in 409 and *Oedipus at Kolonos,* staged posthumously in 401. Some evidence suggests that *Antigone* was produced around 442–441 and *Oedipus the King* in the 420s. *Aias*, *Elektra*, and *Women of Trakhis* have been conjecturally, but never conclusively, dated through stylistic analysis. Aristotle, who had access we forever lack to the hundreds of fifth-century plays produced at the Dionysia, preferred Sophocles to his rivals Aeschylus and Euripides. He considered *Oedipus the King* the perfect example of tragic form, and developed his theory of tragedy from his analysis of it.

Sophocles' fellow citizens respected him sufficiently to vote him into high city office on at least three occasions. He served for a year as chief tribute-collector for Athens' overseas empire. A controversial claim by Aristophanes of Byzantium, in the third century, implies that Sophocles' tribe was so impressed by a production of *Antigone* that they voted him in as one of ten military generals (*strategoi*) in 441–440. Later in life Sophocles was respected as a participant in democratic governance at the highest level. In 411 he was elected to a ten-man commission charged with replacing Athens' discredited democratic governance with an oligarchy, a development that followed the military's catastrophic defeat in Sicily in 413.

Most ancient biographical sources attest to Sophocles' good looks, his easygoing manner, and his enjoyment of life. Athanaeus' multivolume *Deipnosophistai*, a compendium of gossip and dinner chat about and among ancient worthies, includes several vivid passages that reveal Sophocles as both a commanding presence and an impish prankster, ready one moment to put down a schoolmaster's boorish literary criticism and the next to flirt with the wine boy.

Sophocles is also convincingly described as universally respected, with amorous inclinations and intensely religious qualities that, to his contemporaries, did not seem incompatible. Religious piety meant something quite different to an Athenian than the humility, sobriety, and aversion to sensual pleasure it might suggest to us—officially, if not actually. His involvement in various cults, including one dedicated to a god of health and another to the hero Herakles, contributed to his reputation as "loved by the gods" and "the most religious of men." He was celebrated—and worshipped after his death as a hero—for bringing a healing cult (related to Aesculapius and involving a snake) to Athens. It is possible he founded an early version of a hospital. He never flinched from portraying the Greek gods as often wantonly cruel, destroying innocent people, for instance, as punishment for their ancestors' crimes. But the gods in *Antigone*, *Oedipus at Kolonos*, and *Philoktetes* mete out justice with a more even hand.

One remarkable absence in Sophocles' own life was documented suffering of any kind. His luck continued to the moment his body was placed in its tomb. As he lay dying, a Spartan army had once again invaded the Athenian countryside, blocking access to Sophocles' burial site beyond Athens' walls. But after Sophocles' peaceful death the Spartan general allowed the poet's burial party to pass through his lines, apparently out of respect for the god Dionysos.

Robert Bagg

James Scully

NOTE

1. Unless otherwise indicated, the line numbers and note numbers for translations of Sophocles' dramas other than *Antigone* refer to those in the Harper Perennial *Complete Sophocles* series.

Antigone

"FROM WHAT KIND OF PARENTS WAS I BORN?"

*A*ntigone opens just before dawn in Thebes, on the day after the city's defenders have repelled a massive assault by fighters from seven Argive cities. The Argive objective had been to return the Theban throne to Poly neikes, elder son of Oedipus. But Polyneikes and his younger brother, Eteokles, Thebes' reigning king, killed each other with simultaneous spear-thrusts during the failed assault.[1] Antigone, the sister of the slain men, returns fierce and agitated from the battlefield with news for their sister Ismene: Kreon has just become Thebes' ruler following the deaths of his two nephews. He has apparently already honored and buried the loyal Eteokles, but has vilified Polyneikes for attacking his own city and now forbids his burial. Antigone declares she will bury her brother, no matter what it costs her.

Antigone thrived throughout the twentieth century as the perfect ancient play to dramatize rebellion against tyrants. Kreon could be costumed and directed to represent any number of oppressors, and Antigone's fearless eloquence inflected to expose their evil and banality. Productions have reimagined her as a martyred fighter in various righteous causes: she's been a member of the French resistance, the sister of an IRA terrorist or an Argentinean *desaparacido*, and a Vietnam War resister. Antigone will undoubtedly be drafted to face down tyrants yet unborn.

There's a downside, however, to interpreting *Antigone* solely through its capacity for embodying contemporary political battles. None of the play's clashes is as clear-cut, or its characters as consistent, as they first seem. (Thebes' resident prophet—Tiresias, who appears in a single scene as the play's most commanding figure and who delivers an unambiguous condemnation of Kreon—is the sole exception.) Kreon, for instance, addressing his aristocratic peers hours after assuming power, reassuringly articulates his democratic principles and policies. He promises to accept good advice, act on it, avoid and denounce policies that would lead Thebes to destruction, and punish any citizen who betrays Thebes, including his traitorous and deceased nephew. But Kreon will fail to follow every one of his precepts. In the end, the consequences of his own actions will even force him to order a proper burial for Polyneikes. A look into Kreon's soul to locate his core beliefs—opening him up like a wax writing tablet in its case, to paraphrase Kreon's son Haimon—would reveal his moral emptiness. As Kreon puts his crowd-pleasing but insincere inaugural speech behind him, he acts on intense and ugly prejudices, not principles.

Antigone, who possesses both character and principle in abundance, also has suppressed something of her nature in order to steel herself against Kreon's power and arrogance. She will accept nothing less than giving Polyneikes his full burial rights and will welcome her own death, if that's what it takes.

But as she elaborates her view of the world, she reveals the life-suppressing extremity of her allegiances. The deaths of her parents and brothers have made her passionate to rejoin them in Hades. But when actually facing death, Antigone suddenly yearns for the marriage and childbearing she has denied herself. The number and decisiveness of his characters' reversals suggest that Sophocles views human nature as often unsure or unaware of its own deepest desires. As the pressure of catastrophic events increases, sudden surges of desire reveal the major characters' contradictions, their second thoughts, and their consequent desperation. The conflicted Guard, who debates whether it's safe or suicidal to bring Kreon the bad news that Polyneikes' body has been illegally buried, comically prefigures Sophocles' encompassing vision: events can overpower the persons mortals think they are. Staging *Antigone* exclusively to unsettle contemporary political orthodoxies risks turning a blazing but nuanced play into propaganda.

Greek dramatists in the fifth century BCE, and certainly Sophocles, did in fact reflect the impact of political issues in their plays, though they did so invariably by shaping an ancient myth to illuminate their audience's present-day concerns. This strategy both aroused and distanced emotional response. *Antigone* itself, for instance, has at its core a bitter and sometimes deadly public issue in Athenian life: the burial of war casualties. Athens' pro-war ruling party had tried to suppress the resentment of the bereaved and limit mourning of fallen soldiers to a once-a-year ceremony at which a chosen orator gave a patriotic speech. The women of Athens resented both the wars and the deprivation of their chance to give their dead proper burials.

Aristophanes, who was, like most of his fellow aristocrats, anti-war, turns their resentment into a full-scale comic rebellion in *Lysistrata*.

Though Sophocles is wholly sympathetic to Antigone's rebellion and her contempt for Kreon, he shows us she still possesses desires and emotions normal to a woman. As she faces death, she feels these intensely and expresses them in her farewell speeches. *Antigone*, as it unfolds, has become less about dictatorship and honoring the dead than about love's destructive powers.

In the play's opening scene, Antigone explains to Ismene how and why she must bury her brother:

> I'll bury Polyneikes myself. I'll do
> what's honorable, and then I'll die.
> I who love him will lie down
> next to him who loves me—
> my criminal conduct blameless!—
> for I owe more to the dead, with whom
> I will spend a much longer time,
> than I will ever owe to the living.   (85–92)

The Greek verb Antigone uses for "lie down," *keisomai*, is equally appropriate to describe lying down in death (either before burial or in Hades) or having sexual relations with a lover. The English phrase, of course, has a similar range. The words she uses to describe their kinship, *philê* with *philou* (translated here as "I who love him" next to "him who loves me"), accentuate both the emotional bond and the comforting physical proximity of siblings.[2] The Greek words translated as "my criminal conduct blameless," *hosia panourgesas* (literally, "sacred transgressions"), refer primarily to the outlawed act of burying her "traitor" brother, but as some scholars have argued, they could also suggest, given the way they are embedded in the sentence, incestuous love. They may convey simply a sister's need to embrace her brother. Her family's incestuous history does haunt Antigone, as she says at lines 946–949. If Sophocles did intend the erotic implication, it allows him to heighten Antigone's passionate feelings for her dead brother beyond any conventional intrafamilial love. Antigone ends this conversation with Ismene by permanently disowning her cautious sister for refusing to help, and then she heads to the battlefield alone.

When, after performing the forbidden rituals, Antigone is caught, she admits and then fiercely defends her crime, citing immutable laws of *philia* that require a family to bury and honor its dead. Unmoved, Kreon condemns her to die, confident that only those who support Thebes may claim true *philia*. The Greek conception of *philia*, which involves the loyalty and affection binding friends and loved ones in one community, and the city and its citizens in another, will become a central battleground in the play. In the following lines Kreon and Antigone each invoke *philia* to justify their position:

Kreon   The brave deserve better than the vile.
Antigone Who knows what matters to the dead?
Kreon   Not even death reconciles enemies.
Antigone I made no enemies by being born!
                   I made my lifelong friends at birth.

Kreon   Then go down to them! Love your dead brothers!

                                                                    (564–569)

Shared birth parents and nothing else, Antigone declares, determines her *philoi* (friends and loved ones) for life. Audiences (and Kreon, of course) know Antigone and her siblings were born of incestuous sexual intercourse, and that the pollution incurred is sure to pass from one generation to the next. Kreon's taunt, that she should "go down to" her dead brothers, resonates with disgust—not only for her lack of shame but because it infuriates Kreon that his son Haimon plans to marry this distasteful rebel. When Haimon arrives to defend Antigone, Kreon denounces her as both a traitor and an unsuitable wife, warning Haimon that she will be spiteful in the house and frigid in bed. Love now takes center stage. A choral hymn to the power of Eros and Aphrodite immediately follows the father-son conflict. Addressing Eros directly, they sing:

> And those you seize go mad.
>
> You wrench even good men's minds
> so far off course they crash in ruins.
> Now you ignite hatred in men
> of the same blood—but allure flashing
> from the keen eyes of the bride
> always wins, for Desire wields
> all the power of ancient law:
> Aphrodite the implacable
> plays cruel games with our lives.   (871–880)

Antigone's outward expression of erotic feeling remains limited to her fleeting wish, in the first scene, to embrace the dead Polyneikes. She never acknowledges that she is betrothed to Haimon, or so much as mentions his name. She pursues a different commitment: "Long ago / I dedicated [my life] to the dead" (604–605). Although she never abandons this dedication, she soon dramatizes both its costs and its ironies. Just before she's led away to be entombed in a cave, Antigone (who might have changed her costume and returned to the stage wearing a bridal gown) reaches up to lift her veil, uncovering her whole head and addressing the Chorus: "Look at me, princely citizens of Thebes" (1032). This gesture echoes the climactic moment of a traditional Greek marriage celebration: after the bride exposes her face to all in attendance, the groom lifts her onto a mule cart (or chariot) that carries them to his family home and the nuptial bed. Antigone, however, announces she will consummate an anti-marriage, one she achingly describes:

> Hades, who chills each one of us to sleep,
> will guide me down to Acheron's shore.
> I'll go hearing no wedding hymn
> to carry me to my bridal chamber, or songs
> girls sing when flowers crown a bride's hair;
> I'm going to marry the River of Pain.   (890–895)

Her perplexed outburst "From what kind of parents was I born?" (950) recalls Oedipus' sweeping denunciation of marriage in *Oedipus the King* (1591–1596). She has always known that her parents' incestuous marriage will have an evil impact on her. Since in ancient Greek culture only the women were blamed for incestuous sexual relationships, even if men or gods initiate them, she attributes her family's curse solely to her mother's "horrendous . . . coupling" with her father (948–949).

Kreon, an extended member of this family, seems cursed as well. Not until Tiresias appears does Kreon understand how wrong he was to oppose Antigone. Thebes' perennial prophet denounces Kreon in both secular and religious terms:

> You have thrown children from the sunlight
> down to the shades of Hades, ruthlessly
> housing a living person in a tomb,
> while you detain here, among us, something
> that belongs to the gods who live below
> our world—the naked unwept corpse you've robbed
> of the solemn grieving we owe our dead.
> None of this should have been any concern
> of yours—or of the Olympian gods—
> but you have involved them in your outrage!
> Therefore, avengers wait to ambush you—
> the Furies sent by Hades and its gods
> will punish you for the crimes I have named.
>   (1180–1192)

Kreon himself rushes to release Antigone. But it's too late. Haimon, next to Antigone's corpse, lunges to kill his father, misses, and then falls on his own sword. Hearing the news, Kreon's wife runs into the palace and kills herself, thrusting a blade into her side. The play continues to its swift conclusion with Kreon's belated self-castigation. Antigone, as she predicted, receives no mourning from what's left of her Theban royal family. Her absence, during the play's final scene, from Kreon's and the Elders' remorse, is a masterstroke. The damage that their denial of her passion has inflicted on the Theban community is bitter testimony enough to her courage and its cost.

NOTES

1. Eteokles is never named as the king whom Kreon succeeds, but it is implicit in 203–206.

2. Winnington-Ingram (92–116) has explored erotic passion's decisive impact on the characters' actions as well as its powerful presence in several choral odes.

Antigone

CHARACTERS

ANTIGONE, daughter of Oedipus

ISMENE, daughter of Oedipus

ELDERS of Thebes (Chorus)

LEADER of the Chorus

KREON, king of Thebes, uncle of Antigone,
    Polyneikes, and Eteokles

GUARD

Kreon's Men

HAIMON, son of Kreon

TIRESIAS, prophet of Thebes

Lad

MESSENGER

EURYDIKE, wife of Kreon

*It is dawn in front of KREON's palace in Thebes, the day after the battle
in which the Theban defenders repelled an attack on the city by an
Argive coalition that included the rebel Polyneikes, elder son of Oedipus.
Polyneikes and his younger brother, Eteokles, who has remained loyal to
Thebes, have killed each other simultaneously in face-to-face combat at
one of Thebes' seven gates. KREON has suddenly seized the throne. In dim,
streaky light, ANTIGONE runs from offstage and calls out ISMENE's name.
ISMENE enters through the central doors.*

ANTIGONE

Ismene, love! My own kind! Born
like me from that same womb!
Can you think of one evil—
of all those Oedipus started—
that Zeus hasn't used *our own lives*
to finish? There's nothing—no pain,
no shame, no terror, no humiliation!—
you and I haven't seen and shared.
Now there's this new command
our commander in chief   10
imposes on the whole city—
do you know about it?
Have you heard? *You don't know,*
do you? It threatens our loved ones
as if they were our enemies!

*ANTIGONE is out of breath. ISMENE is startled but slow to comprehend the
reason for her sister's agitation.*

ISMENE

Not a word about our family has reached *me*,
Antigone—encouraging or horrible.
Not since we sisters lost our brothers
on the day their hands struck
the double blow that killed them both.   20
And since the Argive army fled last night
I've not heard anything that could improve
our luck—or make it any worse.

ANTIGONE
>   That's what I thought.
And why I've brought you out past the gates—
where no one else can hear what I say.

ISMENE
>   What's wrong?
It's plain something *you've heard* makes you livid.

ANTIGONE
It's Kreon. The way he's treated our brothers.
Hasn't he buried one with honor?
But he's shamed the other. Disgraced him!
Eteokles, they say, was laid to rest   30
according to law and custom.
The dead will respect him in Hades.
But Polyneikes' sorry body can't be touched.

The city is forbidden to mourn him or bury him
—no tomb, no tears. Convenient forage
for cruising birds to feast their fill.
That's the clear order our good general
gives you and me—yes, I said me!
They say he's coming here to proclaim it
in person to those who haven't heard it.   40

This is not something he takes lightly.
Violate any provision—the sentence is
you're stoned to death in your own city.

Now you know.
                    And soon you'll prove
how nobly born you really are.
Or did our family breed a coward?

ISMENE

If that's the bind we're in, you poor thing,
what good can *I* do by yanking the knot
tighter—*or* by trying to pry it loose?

ANTIGONE

Make up your mind. Will you join me?   50
Share the burden?

ISMENE

                    At what risk? What are you asking?

ANTIGONE

(raising up her hands)
Will you help these hands lift his body?

ISMENE

You want to bury him? Break the law?

ANTIGONE

I'm going to bury my brother—your brother!—
with or without your help. I won't betray him.

ISMENE

You scare me, Sister. Kreon's forbidden this.

ANTIGONE

He's got *no right* to keep me from what's mine!

ISMENE

(raising her voice)

He's mine too!

            Just think what our father's

destruction meant for us both.

Because of those horrible deeds—   60

all self-inflicted, all self-detected—

he died hated and notorious,

his eyes battered into blindness

by his own hands. And then

his wife and mother—two roles

for one woman—disposed

of her life with a noose

of twisted rope. And now

our poor brothers die the same day

in a mutual act of kin murder!   70

Think how much worse

our own deaths will be—abandoned

as we are—if we defy the king's

proclamation and his power.

Remember, we're women. How

can we fight men? They're stronger.

We must accept these things—and worse to come.

I want the Spirits of the Dead

to understand this: I'm not free.

I must obey whoever's in charge.   80

It's crazy to attempt the impossible!

ANTIGONE

Then I'll stop asking you! And if you change
your mind, I won't accept your help.
Go be the person you've chosen to be.
I'll bury Polyneikes myself. I'll do
what's honorable, and then I'll die.
I who love him will lie down
next to him who loves me—
my criminal conduct blameless!—
for I owe more to the dead, with whom   90
I will spend a much longer time,
than I will ever owe to the living.
Go ahead, please yourself—defy
laws the gods expect us to honor.

ISMENE

I'm not insulting them! But how can I
defy the city? I don't have the strength.

ANTIGONE

Then make that your excuse. I'll heal
with earth the body of the brother I love.

ISMENE

I feel so sorry for you. And afraid.

ANTIGONE

Don't waste your fear. Straighten out your own life.   100

ISMENE

At least tell nobody what you're planning!
Say nothing about it. And neither will I.

ANTIGONE

No! Go on, tell them all!
I will hate you much more for your silence—
if you don't shout it everywhere.

ISMENE

You're burning to do what should stop you cold.

ANTIGONE

One thing I do know: I'll please those who matter.

ISMENE

As if you could! You love fights you can't win.

ANTIGONE

When my strength is exhausted, I'll quit.

ISMENE

Hopeless passion is wrong from the start.   110

ANTIGONE

Say that again and I'll despise you.
So will the dead—and they'll hate you
far longer. But go! Let me and my
recklessness deal with this alone.

No matter what I suffer
I won't die dishonored.

Exit ANTIGONE *toward open country;* ISMENE *calls out her next lines as her
sister leaves, then she enters the palace through the great central doors.*

ISMENE

If you're determined, go ahead.
And know this much: you are a fool
to attempt this, but you're loved all
the more by the family you love.   120

Chorus of Theban ELDERS *enters singing.*

ELDERS

Morning sunlight, loveliest ever
to shine on seven-gated Thebes!
Day's golden eye, risen at last
over Dirke's glittering waters!
You stampede the Argive!
Invading in full battle gear,
his white shield flashing, he's wrenched
by your sharp piercing bit
headlong into retreat!
This attacker who championed   130
quarrelsome Polyneikes
skimmed through our farmland—
a white-feathered Eagle
screeching, horsehair

flaring from the helmets
of well-armed troops.

He had circled our houses, threatening
all seven gates, his spearpoints
out for blood, but he was thrown back
before his jaws could swell   140
with our gore, before the Firegod's
incendiary pine tar
engulfed the towers ringing our walls.
He cannot withstand the harsh blare
of battle that roars up
around him—as our Dragon
wrestles him down.

How Zeus hates a proud tongue!
And when this river of men
surged forward, with arrogance   150
loud as its flash of gold,
he struck—with his own lightning—
that firebrand shouting in triumph
from the battlements!
Free-falling from the mad
fury of his charge, torch
still in his hand,
he crashed to earth, the man
who'd turned on us the raving
blast of his loathsome words.   160
But threats stuck in his throat:

to each enemy soldier
Ares the brute wargod,
our surging wheelhorse,
assigned a separate doom,
shattering every attack.

Now seven captains guarding seven gates—
our captains facing theirs—
throw down their arms as trophies
for Zeus—all but the doomed pair   170
born to one father, one mother,
who share even their death—
when their twin spears drive home.

Victory is now ours!
Her name is pure glory,
her joy resounds
through Thebes' own joy—Thebes
swarming with chariots!
Let us now banish
this war from our minds   180
and visit each god's temple,
singing all night long! May
Bakkhos, the god whose dancing
rocks Thebes, be there to lead us!

Enter KREON.

LEADER

(sotto voce to his fellow ELDERS)

Enter our new king,
Kreon, the son of Menoikeus,
who came to power
abruptly, when the gods changed our luck.
What plans does he turn over
in his mind—what will he ponder   190
with this Council of the Wise
summoned in his new role?

KREON

Men, we have just survived some rough weather.
Monstrous waves have battered our city,
but now the gods have steadied the waters.
I sent my servants to gather you here
because, of all my people, I know
your veneration for Laios' royal
power has never wavered. When Oedipus
ruled our city, and then was struck down, you   200
stood by his sons. Now both have fallen
together, killed in one lethal exchange.

Because each struck the other's deathblow, each
was defiled by his own brother's blood.
As nearest kin to the men killed,
I've taken power and assumed the throne.

You cannot measure a man's character,
policies, or his common sense—until
you see him at work enforcing old laws
and making new ones. To me, there's nothing   210

worse than a man, while he's running a city,
who fails to act on sound advice—but fears
something so much his mouth clamps shut.
Nor have I any use for a man whose friend
means more to him than his country.
Believe me, Zeus, for you miss nothing,
I'll always speak out when I see Thebes choose
destruction rather than deliverance.
I'll never think our country's enemy
can be my friend. Keep this in mind: 220
our *country* is the ship that must keep us safe.
It's only on board her, among the men
who sail her upright, that we make true friends.

Such are the principles I will follow
to preserve Thebes' greatness. Akin to these
are my explicit orders concerning
Oedipus' sons: Eteokles, who died
fighting for our city, and who excelled
in combat, will be given the rituals
and burial proper to the noble dead.   230

But his brother—I mean Polyneikes, who
returned from exile utterly determined
to burn down his own city, incinerate
the gods we worship, revel in kinsmen's blood,
enslave everyone left alive—
as for him, it is now a crime for Thebans
to bury him or mourn him. Dogs and birds
will savage and outrage his corpse—

an ugly and a visible disgrace.
That is my thinking. And I will never   240
tolerate giving a bad man more respect
than a good one. Only those faithful to Thebes
will I honor—in this life and after death.

LEADER

That is your pleasure, Kreon: punish Thebes'
betrayers and reward her defenders.
You have all the authority you need
to discipline the living and the dead.

KREON

Are you willing to help enforce this law?

LEADER

Ask someone younger to shoulder that burden.

KREON

But I've already posted men at the corpse.   250

LEADER

Then what instructions do you have for me?

KREON

Don't join the cause of those who break this law.

LEADER

Who but a fool would want to die?

KREON

Exactly. He'd be killed. But easy money
frequently kills those it deludes.

Enter GUARD. *He tends to mime the actions he describes.*

GUARD

I didn't run here at such a breakneck
pace, King, that I'm winded. Pausing to think
stopped me, wheeled me around, headed me back
more than once. My mind kept yelling at me:
"Reckless fool—why go where you'll be punished?"   260
Then: "Lazy clod! Dawdling, are you? What if
Kreon hears this news from somebody else?—
you'll pay for it."
                    I made myself dizzy,
hurrying slowly, stretching out a short road.
I finally realized I had to come.
If I'm talking annihilation here,
I'll still say it, since I'm of the opinion
nothing but my own fate can cause me harm.

KREON

What's making you so agitated?

GUARD

The need to explain my role in this matter.   270
I didn't do it, I didn't see who did.
So it wouldn't be right to punish me.

KREON

You're obsessed with protecting yourself.
That's a nice fortified wall you've thrown up
around your news—which must be odd indeed.

GUARD

You bet. And bad news must be broken slowly.

KREON

Why not just tell it? Then you can vanish.

GUARD

But I *am* telling you! That corpse—someone's
buried it and run off. They sprinkled thirsty
dust on it. Then did all the rituals.   280

KREON

What are you saying? What man would dare do this?

GUARD

I've no idea. No marks from a pickax,
no dirt thrown up by a shovel. The ground's
all hard and dry, unbroken—no wheel ruts.
Whoever did this left no trace.
When the man on dawn-watch showed it to us,
we all got a nasty surprise. The dead man
had dropped out of sight. He wasn't buried,
but dusted over, as though someone had tried
to stave off defilement. There was no sign   290
dogs or wild animals had chewed the corpse.

Then we all started yelling rough words, threats,
blaming each other, every guard ready
to throw punches—nobody to stop us.
All of us under suspicion—but none
of us convicted. We all denied it—
swearing to god we'd handle red-hot iron
or walk through fire to back up our oaths.

After interrogation got us nowhere,
one man spoke up and made us hang our heads   300
toward the ground in terror. We couldn't do
what he said—or avoid trouble if we did.
He advised us to tell you what happened,
not try to hide it. That seemed our best move.
So we drew lots to choose the messenger.
I lost. I'm no happier to be here
than you are to see me. Don't I know that.
Nobody loves the man who brings bad news.

LEADER

King, something has been bothering me: suppose
this business was inspired by the gods?   310

KREON

Stop! Before your words fill me with rage.
Now, besides sounding old, you sound senile.
How could anyone possibly believe
the gods protect this corpse? Did *they* cover
his nakedness to reward him for loyal

service—this man who came here to burn
their colonnaded temples and treasuries,
to wipe out their country and tear up its laws?
Do you think that the gods honor rebels?
They don't. But for a good while now   320
men who despise me have been muttering
under their breaths. My edict bruised their necks.
They were rebelling against a just yoke—
unlike you good citizens who support me.
I'm sure these malcontents bribed my sentries
to do what they did.

       Mankind's most deadly
invention is money. It plunders cities,
encourages men to abandon their homes,
tempts honest people to do shameful things.
It instructs them in criminal practice,   330
drives them to act on every godless impulse.
By doing this for silver, these men have
guaranteed that, sooner or later,
they'll pay the price.

(addressing the GUARD)

      But you who worship Zeus—
since Zeus enforces his own will through mine—
be sure of this, it is my solemn oath:
if you don't find the man who carried out
this burial and drag him before me,
a quick trip to Hades won't be your fate.
All of you will be strung up—and you'll hang   340
for a while, your insolence on display.

From then on, you may calculate exactly
how much profit to expect from your crimes.
More men are destroyed by ill-gotten wealth
than such "wealth" ever saved from destruction.

GUARD

May I speak further? Or shall I just leave?

KREON

Don't you realize that your words pain me?

GUARD

Do your ears ache, or does the pain go deeper?

KREON

Why does the source of my pain interest you?

GUARD

I only sting your ears. The man   350
who did this stabs your gut.

KREON

You've run off at the mouth since you were born.

GUARD

Maybe so. But I had no part in this crime.

KREON

I think you did. Sold your life for some coins.

GUARD

It's a sad thing when a judge gets it wrong.

KREON

You'll soon be on the wrong end of a judgment
yourself.
            If you don't find the guilty one,
you'll find your greed buys you nothing but grief.

GUARD

I hope he's caught, but Fate will decide that.
And you'll never see me coming back here.   360
Now that I have been spared—when everything
seemed so desperate—all I can think about
is how much gratitude I owe the gods.

Exit GUARD to open country; KREON enters his palace.

ELDERS

Wonders abound, but none
more astounding than man!
He crosses to the far side
of white seas, blown
by winter gales, sailing
below huge waves.
He wears Earth down—   370
our primal, eternal,
inexhaustible god,
his stallion-sired mules

plowing her soil
back and forth
year after year.

All breeds of carefree
bird, savage beast,
and deep-sea creature,
ingenious man   380
snares in his woven nets.
He drives the mountain herds
from wild lairs down to his folds.
He coaxes rough-maned horses
to thrust their necks through his yoke.
He tames the tireless mountain bull.

He has taught himself speech,
wind-quick thought,
and all the talents
that govern a city—   390
how to take shelter
from cold skies or pelting rain.
Never baffled,
always resourceful,
he accepts every challenge.
But from Hades alone
has he found no way out—
though from hopeless disease
he has found a defense.

Exceeding all expectation,   400
his robust power to create
sometimes brings evil,
at other times, excellence.
When he follows the laws
Earth teaches him—
and Justice, which he's sworn
the gods he will enforce—
he soars with his city.
But reckless and corrupt,
a man will be driven   410
from his nation disgraced.

Let no man guilty of such things
share my hearth or invade my thoughts.

Enter GUARD, from countryside, leading ANTIGONE.

LEADER
I'm stunned—what's this? A warning from the gods?
I know this girl. She is Antigone.
Don't we all recognize her?
Unlucky Oedipus was her father.
And now her own luck runs out.
What's happening? You—under guard?
Are you a prisoner? Did you break   420
the king's law? Commit some thoughtless act?

GUARD

There's your perpetrator. We caught her
burying the corpse. Where's Kreon?

Enter KREON.

LEADER

Here he comes. Just in time.

KREON

What makes my arrival so timely?

GUARD

Sir, never promise something won't happen.
Second thoughts can make your first one a lie.
I vowed I'd never come back here,
after you tongue-lashed me with those threats.
Then came a pleasure like no other,   430
because it's a total surprise, something
we hope for but can't believe will happen.
So I came back—though I swore I wouldn't—
to bring you the girl we caught sprinkling dust
on the dead body. No need to throw dice.
This time the good fortune was all mine.
Now she's all yours. Question and convict her.
Do as you see fit. But I have the right
to go free of trouble once and for all.

KREON

Your prisoner—where was she when captured?   440

GUARD

Covering up the dead body. There you have it.

KREON

Do you know what you just said? No mistake?

GUARD

I saw her bury the man you said no one
could bury. How can I say it plainer?

KREON

How did you see her? Was she caught in the act?

GUARD

Here's what happened. We went back there
after those ugly threats of yours, to brush
the dirt off the body and strip it down
to its rotting flesh. Afterwards, we hunkered
upwind under some hills to spare us any stench   450
the body might have sent our way. Each man
kept alert, and kept his neighbor alert,
by raking him with outbursts of abuse
if he seemed to neglect his watch.
We kept at it until the round sun had climbed
the heavens and baked us in the noon heat.
Then, rising from the earth, a whirlwind

whipped up the dust, and terror filled the sky,
choking the grasslands, tearing leaves off trees,
churning up grit all around us.

                                  Our eyes squeezed shut,   460
we waited out this god-sent pestilence.
After a bit the dust cleared, and we saw her
cry out in anguish, a piercing scream
like a bird homing to find her nest robbed.
When she saw the body stripped naked,
she wailed one more time, then yelled a string
of curses at those who'd done it. She scooped up
powdery dust and, from a graceful bronze
urn, poured out three cool swallows for the dead.
Soon as we saw this, we moved in to stop her.   470
She wasn't a bit shocked when we charged her
with the earlier crime, and now this one.
Didn't deny a thing. That pleased,
but also troubled me. Escaping blame
oneself is always a relief. Still, it hurts
to cause your own people grief. But all that
matters much less to me than my own safety.

KREON

(to ANTIGONE)

You! Don't stand there nodding your head.
Out with it! Admit this or deny it.

ANTIGONE

I swear I did. And I don't deny it.   480

KREON

(to GUARD)

You are excused from this grim business.
You're now free to go anywhere you please.

Exit GUARD. KREON turns to ANTIGONE.

Explain something to me without elaborating.
Were you aware of my decree forbidding this?

ANTIGONE

Of course I knew. We all knew.

KREON

And still you dared to violate the law?

ANTIGONE

I did. It wasn't *Zeus* who issued me
this order. And Justice—who lives below—
was not involved. They'd never condone it!
I deny that your edicts—since *you,* a mere man,   490
imposed them—have the force to trample on
the gods' unwritten and infallible laws.
Their laws are not ephemeral—they weren't
made yesterday. They will rule forever.
No man knows how far back in time they go.
I'd never let any man's arrogance
bully me into breaking the gods' laws.
I'll die someday—how could I not know that?
I knew it without your proclamation.

If I do die young, that's an advantage,   500
for doesn't a person like me, who lives
besieged by trouble, escape by dying?
My own death isn't going to bother me,
but I would be devastated to see
my mother's son die and rot unburied.
I've no regrets for what I've done. And if you
consider my acts foolhardy, I say:
look at the fool charging me with folly.

LEADER

It's apparent this girl's nature is savage
like her father's. She hasn't got the sense   510
to back off when she gets into trouble.

KREON

Stubborn spirits are the first to crack.
It's always the iron tool hardened by fire
that snaps and shatters. And headstrong horses
can be tamed by a little iron bit.
There's no excuse for a slave
to preen when her master's home.
This girl learned insolence long before
she broke this law. What's more, she keeps on
insulting us, and then gloats about it.   520
There is no doubt that if she emerges
victorious, and is never punished,
I am no man. *She* will be the man here.

I don't care if she is my sister's child,
a blood relative, closer than all those
who worship Zeus in my household,
she—and her sister—still must die.
I charge her sister too with conspiring
to bury Polyneikes. Bring her out.
I observed her inside just now,   530
screaming, hysterical, deranged.
Someone who intends to commit a crime
can lose control of a guilty conscience.
Her furtive treason gives itself away.

Two of Kreon's Men enter the palace. KREON turns back to ANTIGONE.

But I also hate it when someone caught
red-handed tries to glorify her crime.

ANTIGONE

Take me and kill me—is that your whole plan?

KREON

That's it. When that's done I'll be satisfied.

ANTIGONE

Then what stops you? Are you waiting for me
to accept what you've said? I never will.   540
And nothing I say will ever please you.
Yet, since you did mention glory, how
could I do anything more glorious

than build my own brother a tomb?
These men here would approve my actions—
if fear didn't seal their lips.
                              Tyranny
is fortunate in many ways: it can,
for instance, say and do anything it wants.

KREON

These Thebans don't see it your way.

ANTIGONE

But they do. To please you they bite their tongues.   550

KREON

Aren't you ashamed not to follow their lead?

ANTIGONE

Since when is it shameful to honor a brother?

KREON

You had another brother who died fighting him?

ANTIGONE

That's right. Born to the same mother and father.

KREON

Then why do you honor Polyneikes
when doing so desecrates Eteokles?

ANTIGONE

Eteokles wouldn't agree with you.

KREON

Oh, but he would. Because you've honored
treason as though it were patriotism.

ANTIGONE

It was his *brother* who died, not his *slave*!   560

KREON

That brother died ravaging our country!
Eteokles fell fighting to protect it.

ANTIGONE

Hades will still expect his rituals!

KREON

The brave deserve better than the vile.

ANTIGONE

Who knows what matters to the dead?

KREON

Not even death reconciles enemies.

ANTIGONE

I made no enemies by being born!
I made my lifelong friends at birth.

KREON

Then go down to them! Love your dead brothers!
While I'm alive, no woman governs me.   570

Enter ISMENE, led in by Kreon's Men.

LEADER

Ismene's coming from the palace.
She cries the loving tears of a sister.
Her eyes fill up, her flushed face darkens.
Tears pour down her cheeks.

KREON

                              Now you—a viper
who slithered through my house, quietly
drinking my blood! I never knew
I nurtured *two* insurrections,
both attacking my throne.
                              Go ahead,
confess your role in this burial
party. Or do you claim ignorance?   580

ISMENE

I confess it—if she'll let me.
I accept my full share of the blame.

ANTIGONE

Justice won't let you make that claim, Sister!
You refused to help me. You took no part.

ISMENE

You're leaving on a grim voyage. I'm not
ashamed to suffer with you the whole way.

ANTIGONE

The dead in Hades know who buried him.
I don't want love that just shows up in words.

ISMENE

You'll disgrace me, Sister! Don't keep me
from honoring our dead! Take me with you!   590

ANTIGONE

Don't try to share my death! Don't try to claim
you helped me bury him! My death's enough.

ISMENE

With you dead, why would I want to live?

ANTIGONE

Ask Kreon that! You sprang to his defense.

ISMENE

Why do you wound me? It does you no good.

ANTIGONE

I'm sorry if my scorn for him hurts you.

ISMENE

I can still help you. Tell me what to do.

ANTIGONE

Go on living. I'd rather you survived.

ISMENE

Then you want to exclude me from your fate?

ANTIGONE

You made the choice to live. I chose to die.   600

ISMENE

And I've told you how much I hate that choice.

ANTIGONE

Some think you're right. *Others* will think I am.

ISMENE

Then aren't we both equally wrong?

ANTIGONE

Gather your strength. Your life goes on. Long ago
I dedicated my own to the dead.

KREON

One woman only now shows her madness—
the other's been out of her mind since birth.

ISMENE

King, when you are shattered by grief
your native wit vanishes. It just goes.

KREON

You surely lost your wits when you teamed up   610
with a criminal engaged in a crime.

ISMENE

What would my life be like without her?

KREON

You're living that life now. Hers is over.

ISMENE

Then you're willing to kill your own son's bride?

KREON

Oh yes. He'll find other fields to plow.

ISMENE

No other woman would suit him so well.

KREON

I want no pernicious wives for my son.

ISMENE

Dearest Haimon! How your father hates you!

KREON

Enough! No more talk about this marriage.

ISMENE

You're going to rob your son of his bride?   620

KREON

Hades will cancel their marriage for me.

ISMENE

Then you've made up your mind she will die?

KREON

Both *my* mind and *your* mind. No more delay,
men, take them in. Make sure they behave
like women. Don't let either slip away.
Even the brave will try to run
when they see death coming at them.

Kreon's Men take ANTIGONE and ISMENE inside.

ELDERS

Lucky are those
whose lives
never taste evil!   630
For once the gods
attack a family,
their curse never relents.
It sickens life after life,
rising like a deep

sea swell, a darkness
boiling from below, driven
by the wild stormwinds
of Thrace that churn up
black sand from the seafloor—   640
the battered headlands
moan as the storm pounds in.

I see sorrows that struck
the dead Labdakids long ago
break over their children,
wave on wave of sorrows!
Each generation fails
to protect its own youth—
because a god always hacks
at their roots, draining   650
strength that could set them free.
Now the hope that brightened
over the last rootstock
alive in the house
of Oedipus, in its turn
is struck down—
by the blood-drenched dust
the death gods demand,
by reckless talk,
by Furies in the mind.   660

O Zeus,
what human arrogance
can rival your power?

Neither Sleep,
who beguiles us all,
nor the tireless, god-driven months
overcome it.
        O Monarch
whom time cannot age—
you live in the magical
sunrays of Olympos!   670
One law of yours rules
our own and future time,
just as it ruled the past:
nothing momentous man
achieves will go unpunished.

For Hope is a wanderer
who profits multitudes
but tempts just as many
with light-headed longings—
and a man's failure   680
dawns on him only
when blazing coals
scald his feet.

The man was wise
who said these words:
"Evil seems noble—
early and late—to minds
unbalanced by the gods,
but only for a moment

will such men   690
hold off catastrophe."

Enter HAIMON.

LEADER
(to KREON)
There's Haimon,
the youngest of your sons.
Does he come here enraged
that you've condemned Antigone,
the bride he's been promised,
or in shock that his hopes
for marriage have been crushed?

KREON
We'll soon have an answer
better than any prophet's.   700
My son, now that you've heard
my formal condemnation
of your bride, have you come here
to attack your father?
Or will I be dear to you still,
no matter what I do?

HAIMON
I'm yours, Father. I respect your wisdom.
Show me the straight path, and I'll take it.
I couldn't value any marriage more
than the excellent guidance you give me.   710

KREON

Son, that's exactly how you need to think:
follow your father's orders in all things.
It's the reason men pray for loyal sons
to be born and raised in their houses—
so they can harm their father's enemies
and show his friends respect to match his own.
If a man produces worthless children,
what has he spawned? His grief, his rivals' glee.

Don't throw away your judgment, son,
for the pleasure this woman offers.   720
You'll feel her turn ice-cold in your arms—
you'll feel her scorn in the bedroom. No wound
cuts deeper than poisonous love. So spit
this girl out like the enemy she is.
Let her find a mate in Hades.
I caught her in open defiance—
she alone in the whole city—and I will take
her life, just as I promised. I will not
show myself as a liar to my people.
It is useless for her to harp on the Zeus   730
of family life: if I indulge my own
family in rebelliousness,
I must indulge it everywhere.

A man who keeps his own house in order
will be perceived as righteous by his city.
But if anyone steps out of line, breaks

our laws, thinks he can dictate to his king,
he shouldn't expect any praise from me.
Citizens must obey men in office
appointed by the city, both in minor matters   740
and in the great questions of what is just—
even when they think an action unjust.
Obedient men lead ably and serve well.
Caught in a squall of spears, they hold their ground.
They make brave soldiers you can trust.
Insubordination is our worst crime.
It wrecks cities and empties homes. It breaks
and routs even allies who fight beside us.
Discipline is what saves the lives of all
good people who stay out of trouble.   750
And to make sure we enforce discipline—
never let a woman overwhelm a king.
Better to be driven from power, if it
comes to that, by a man. Then nobody
can say you were beaten by some female.

LEADER

Unless the years have sapped my wits, King,
what you have just said was wisely said.

HAIMON

Father, the gods instill reason in men.
It's the most valuable thing we possess.
I don't have the skill—nor do I want it—   760
to contradict all the things you have said.

Though someone else's perspective might help.
Look, it's not in your nature to notice
what people say and do—and what they don't like.
That harsh look on your face makes men afraid—
no one tells you what you'd rather not hear.
But I hear, unobserved, what people think.
Listen. Thebes aches for this girl. *No person
ever*, they're saying, *less deserved to die—
no one's ever been so unjustly killed*   770
for actions as magnificent as hers.
When her own brother died in that bloodbath
she kept him from lying out there unburied,
fair game for flesh-eating dogs and vultures.
Hasn't she earned, they ask, *golden honor?*
Those are the words they whisper in the shadows.

There's nothing I prize more, Father,
than your welfare.
                    What makes a son prouder
than a father's thriving reputation?
Don't fathers feel the same about their sons?   780

Attitudes are like clothes; you can change them.
Don't think that what you say is always right.
Whoever thinks that he alone is wise,
that he's got a superior tongue and brain,
open him up and you'll find him a blank.
It's never shameful for even a wise man
to keep on learning new things all his life.

Be flexible, not rigid. Think of trees
caught in a raging winter torrent: Those
that bend will survive with all their limbs   790
intact. Those that resist are swept away.
Or take a captain who cleats his mainsheet
down hard, never easing off in a blow—
he'll capsize his ship and go right on sailing,
his rowing benches where his keel should be.
Step back from your anger. Let yourself change.

If I, as a younger man, can offer
a thought, it's this: Yes, it would be better
if men were born with perfect understanding.
But things don't work that way. The best response   800
to worthy advice is to learn from it.

LEADER

King, if he has said anything to ease
this crisis, you had better learn from it.
Haimon, you do the same. You both spoke well.

KREON

So men my age should learn from one of yours?

HAIMON

If I happen to be right, yes! Don't look
at my youth, look at what I've accomplished.

KREON

What? Backing rebels makes you proud?

HAIMON

I'm not about to condone wrongdoing.

KREON

Hasn't *she* been attacked by that disease?   810

HAIMON

Your fellow citizens would deny it.

KREON

Shall Thebans dictate how I should govern?

HAIMON

Listen to yourself. You talk like a boy.

KREON

Should I yield to them—or rule Thebes myself?

HAIMON

It's not a *city* if one man owns it.

KREON

Don't we say men in power *own* their cities?

HAIMON

You'd make a first-rate king of a wasteland.

KREON

It seems this *boy* fights on the woman's side.

HAIMON

Only if you're the woman. You're my concern.

KREON

Then why do you make open war on me?   820

HAIMON

What I attack is your abuse of power.

KREON

Is protecting my interest an abuse?

HAIMON

What is it you protect by scorning the gods?

KREON

Look at yourself! A woman overpowers you.

HAIMON

But no disgraceful impulse ever will.

KREON

Your every word supports that woman.

HAIMON

And you, and me, and the gods of this earth.

KREON

You will not marry her while she's *on* this earth.

HAIMON

Then she will die and, dead, kill someone else.

KREON

You are brazen enough to threaten me?   830

HAIMON

What threatens you is hearing what I think.

KREON

Your mindless attack on me threatens *you*.

HAIMON

I'd question *your* mind if you weren't my father.

KREON

Stop your snide deference! You are her slave.

HAIMON

You're talking at me, but you don't hear me.

KREON

Really? By Olympos above, I hear you.
And I can assure you, you're going to
suffer the consequences of your attacks.

KREON speaks to his Men.

Bring out the odious creature. Let her
die at once in his presence. Let him watch,   840
this bridegroom, as she's killed beside him.

Two of Kreon's Men enter the palace.

HAIMON

Watch her die next to me? You think I'd do that?
Your eyes won't see my face, ever again.
Go on raving to friends who can stand you.

Exit HAIMON.

LEADER

King, the young man's fury hurls him out.
Rage makes a man his age utterly reckless.

KREON

Let him imagine he's superhuman.
He'll never save the lives of those two girls.

LEADER

Then you intend to execute them both?

KREON

Not the one with clean hands.   850
I think you're right about her.

LEADER

The one you plan to kill—how will you do it?

KREON

I will lead her along a deserted road,
and hide her, alive, in a hollow cave.
I'll leave her just enough food to evade
defilement—so the city won't be infected.
She can pray there to Hades, the one god
whom she respects. Maybe he will spare her!
Though she's more likely to learn, in her last hours,
that she's thrown her life away on the dead.   860

*KREON remains onstage during the next choral ode, possibly retiring into
the background.*

ELDERS

Love, you win all
your battles!—raising
havoc with our herds,
dwelling all night
on a girl's soft cheeks,
cruising the oceans,
invading homes
deep in the wilds!
No god can outlast you,
no mortal outrun you.   870
And those you seize go mad.

You wrench even good men's minds
so far off course they crash in ruins.
Now you ignite hatred in men

of the same blood—but allure flashing
from the keen eyes of the bride
always wins, for Desire wields
all the power of ancient law:
Aphrodite the implacable
plays cruel games with our lives.   880

Enter ANTIGONE, dressed in purple as a bride, guarded by Kreon's Men.

LEADER

This sight also drives *me*
outside the law. I can't stop
my own tears flowing when I see
Antigone on her way
to the bridal chamber,
where we all lie down in death.

ANTIGONE

Citizens of our fatherland, you see me
begin my last journey. I take one last look
at sunlight that I'll never see again.
Hades, who chills each one of us to sleep,   890
will guide me down to Acheron's shore.
I'll go hearing no wedding hymn
to carry me to my bridal chamber, or songs
girls sing when flowers crown a bride's hair.
I'm going to marry the River of Pain.

LEADER

Don't praise and glory go with you
to the deep caverns of the dead?
You haven't been wasted by disease.
You've helped no sword earn its keep.
No, you have chosen of your own free will   900
to enter Hades while you're still alive.
No one else has ever done that.

ANTIGONE

I once heard that a Phrygian stranger,
Niobe, the daughter of Tantalos,
died a hideous death on Mount Sipylos.
Living rock, clinging like ivy,
crushed her. Now, people say,
she erodes—rainwater and snow
never leave her alone—they keep on
pouring like tears from her eyes,   910
drenching the clefts of her body.
My death will be like hers,
when the god at last lets me sleep.

LEADER

You forget, child, she was a goddess,
with gods for parents, not a mortal
begotten by mortals like ourselves.
It's no small honor—for a mere woman
to suffer so godlike a fate, in both
how she has lived and the way she will die.

ANTIGONE

Now I'm being laughed at!   920
In the name of our fathers' gods,
wait till I'm gone! Don't mock me
while I stand here in plain sight—
all you rich citizens of this town!

At least I can trust you,
headwaters of the river
Dirke, and you, holy
plains around Thebes, home
of our great chariot-fleet,
to bear me witness: watch them   930
march me off to my strange tomb,
my heaped-up rock-bound prison,
without a friend to mourn me
or any law to protect me—

me, a miserable woman
with no home here on earth
and none down with the dead,
not quite alive, not yet a corpse.

LEADER

You took the ultimate risk when you smashed
yourself against the throne of Justice.   940
But the stiff price you're paying, daughter,
is one you inherit from your father.

ANTIGONE

You've touched my worst grief,
the fate of my father, which I
keep turning over in my mind.
We all were doomed, the whole
grand house of Labdakos,
by my mother's horrendous,
incestuous, coupling with her son.
From what kind of parents was I born?   950

I'm going to them now.
I'm dying unmarried.

And brother Polyneikes,
wasn't yours too a deadly
marriage? And when you
were slaughtered, so was I.

LEADER

Your pious conduct might deserve some praise,
but no assault on power will ever
be tolerated by him who wields it.
It was your own hotheaded   960
willfulness that destroyed you.

ANTIGONE

No friends, no mourners, no wedding songs
go with me. They push me down a road
that runs through sadness.

They have prepared it for me, alone.
Soon I will lose sight of the sun's holy eye,
wretched, with no one to love me,
no one to grieve.

KREON moves forward from the shadows, speaking first to ANTIGONE, *then
to his Men.*

KREON

You realize, don't you, that singing
and wailing would go on forever—if   970
they did the dying any good?

Hurry up now, take her away.
And when you've finished
sealing her off, just as I've ordered,
inside the cave's vault,
leave her there—absolutely
isolated—to decide whether
she wants to die at once, or go
on living in that black hole.
So we'll be pure as far as she's concerned.   980
In either case, today will be the last
she'll ever spend above the ground.

ANTIGONE

My tomb, my bridal bedroom, my home
dug from rock, where they'll keep me forever—
I'll join my family there, so many of us dead,

already welcomed by Persephone.
I'll be the last to arrive, and the worst off,
going down with most of my life unlived.
I hope my coming will please my father,
comfort my mother, and bring joy   990
to you, brother, because I washed your dead
bodies, dressed you with my hands, and poured
blessèd offerings of drink on your graves.
Now, because I honored your corpse,
Polyneikes, *this* is how I'm repaid!
I honored you as wise men would think right.
But I wouldn't have taken that task on
had I been a mother who lost her child,
or if my husband were rotting out there.
For them, I would never defy my city.   1000
You want to know what law lets me say this?
If my husband were dead, I could remarry.
A new husband could give me a new child.
But with my father and mother in Hades,
a new brother could never bloom for me.
That is the law that made me die for you,
Polyneikes. But Kreon says I'm wrong,
terribly wrong. And now I'm his captive.
He pulls me by the wrist to no bride's bed.
I won't hear bridal songs, or feel the joy   1010
of married love, and I will have no share
in raising children. No, I will go grieving,
friendless, and alive to a hollow tomb.
Tell me, gods, which of *your* laws did I break?

I'm too far gone to expect your help.
But whose strength can I count on, when acts
of blessing are considered blasphemy?
If the gods are happy I'm sentenced to die,
I hope one day I'll discover
what divine law I have broken.   1020
But if my judges are at fault, I want *them*
to suffer the pain they inflict on me now.

LEADER

She's still driven by raw gusts
raging through her mind.

KREON

I have no patience with such outbursts.
And none for men who drag their feet.

ANTIGONE

I think you mean my death is near.

KREON

It will be carried out. Don't think otherwise.

ANTIGONE

I leave you, Thebes, city of my fathers.
I leave you, ancient gods. This very moment,   1030
I'm being led away. They cannot wait!

ANTIGONE pulls the veil off her face and shakes her hair free.

Look at me, princely citizens of Thebes:
I'm the last daughter of the kings who ruled you.
Look at what's done to me, and by whom
it's done, to punish me for keeping faith.

Kreon's Men lead ANTIGONE offstage.

ELDERS

Like you, lovely Danaë
endured her loss
of heavenly sunlight
in a brass-bound cell—
a prison secret as a tomb.   1040
Night and day she was watched.
Like yours, my daughter,
her family was a great one.
The seed of Zeus, which fell
on her as golden rain,
she treasured in her womb.
Fate is strange and powerful.
Wealth cannot protect us,
nor can war, high city towers,
or storm-beaten black ships.   1050

Impounded too, was Lycurgos,
short-tempered son of Dryas,
King of Edonia: to pay
him back for insulting
defiance, Dionysos shut

him up in a rocky cell.
There his surging madness ebbed.
He learned too late how mad
he was to taunt this god
with derisive laughter.   1060
When he tried to suppress
Bakkhanalian torches
and women fired by their god,
he angered the Muses,
who love the oboe's song.

By waters off the Black Rocks,
a current joins two seas—
the Bosphoros' channel
follows the Thracian
shoreline of Salmydessos.   1070
Ares from his nearby city
saw this wild assault—
the savage wife of Phineus
attacking his two sons:
her stab-wounds darkened
their vengeance-craving eyes,
burst with a pointed shuttle
gripped in her blood-drenched hands.

Broken spirits, they howled
in their pain—these sons   1080
of a woman unhappy
in her marriage, this daughter

descended from the ancient
Erektheids. Nursed in caves
among her father's storm winds,
this daughter of the gods,
this child of Boreas,
rode swift horses over the mountains—
yet Fate broke her brutally, my child.

Enter TIRESIAS and the Lad who guides him.

TIRESIAS

Theban lords, we walk here side by side,   1090
one pair of eyes looking out for us both.
Blind men must travel with somebody's help.

KREON

What news do you bring, old man Tiresias?

TIRESIAS

I'll tell you. Then you must trust this prophet.

KREON

I've never questioned the advice you've given.

TIRESIAS

And it helped you keep Thebes on a straight course?

KREON

I know your value. I learned it firsthand.

TIRESIAS

Take care.

You're standing on the knife edge of fate.

KREON

What do you mean? That makes me shudder.   1100

TIRESIAS

You'll comprehend when you hear the warnings
issued by my art. When I took my seat
at my accustomed post of augury,
birds from everywhere fluttering nearby,
I heard a strange sound coming from their midst.
They screeched with such mindless ferocity,
any meaning their song possessed was drowned out.
I knew the birds were tearing at each other
with lethal talons. The hovering beats
of thrashing wings could have meant nothing else.   1110
Alarmed, I lit a sacrificial fire,
but the god failed to keep his flames alive.
Then from charred thighbones came a rancid slime,
smoking and sputtering, oozing out
into the ashes. The gallbladder burst open.
Liquefying thighs slid free from the strips
of fat enfolding them.
                          But my attempt
at prophecy failed. The signs I had sought
never appeared—this I learned from my lad.
He's my guide, as I am the guide for others.   1120

Kreon, your mind has sickened Thebes.
Our city's altars, and our city's braziers,
have been defiled, all of them, by dogs
and birds, with flesh torn from the wretched
corpse of Oedipus' fallen son.
Because of this, the gods will not accept
our prayers or the offerings of burnt meat
that come from our hands. No bird now sings
a clear omen—their keen cries have been garbled
by the taste of a slain man's thickened blood.   1130
Think about these facts, son.

                             All men go wrong.
But when a man blunders, he won't be stripped
of his wits and his strength if he corrects
the error he's committed and then ends
his stubborn ways. Stubbornness, you well know,
will bring on charges of stupidity.
Respect the dead. Don't spear the fallen.
How much courage does it take
to kill a dead man?

                     Let me
help you. My counsel is sound and well meant.   1140
No advice is sweeter than that from a wise
source who has only your interests at heart.

KREON

Old man, like archers at target practice,
you all aim arrows at me. And now you
stoop to using prophecy against me.

For a long time I have been merchandise
sold far and wide by you omen-mongers.
Go, make your money, strike your deals, import
silver from Sardis, gold from India,
if it suits you. But you won't hide that corpse   1150
under the earth! Never—even if Zeus'
own eagles fly scraps of flesh to his throne.

Defilement isn't something I fear. It won't
persuade me to order this burial.
I don't accept that men can defile gods.
But even the cleverest of mortals,
venerable Tiresias, will be brought
down hard, if, hoping to turn a profit,
they clothe ugly ideas in handsome words.

TIRESIAS

Does any man grasp . . . does he realize . . .   1160

KREON

Realize . . . what? What point are you making?

TIRESIAS

. . . that no possession is worth more than good sense?

KREON

Just as its absence is our worst disease.

TIRESIAS

But hasn't that disease infected you?

KREON

I won't trade insults with you, prophet.

TIRESIAS

You do when you call my prophecies false.

KREON

Your profession has always loved money.

TIRESIAS

And tyrants have a penchant for corruption.

KREON

You know you're abusing a king in power?

TIRESIAS

You hold power because I helped you save Thebes.   1170

KREON

You're a shrewd prophet. But you love to cause harm.

TIRESIAS

You'll force me to say what's clenched in my heart.

KREON

Say it. Unless you've been paid to say it.

TIRESIAS

I don't think it will pay you to hear it.

KREON

Get one thing straight: my conscience can't be bought.

TIRESIAS

Then tell your conscience this. You will not live
for many circuits of the chariot sun
before you trade a child born from your loins
for all the corpses whose deaths you have caused.
You have thrown children from the sunlight   1180
down to the shades of Hades, ruthlessly
housing a living person in a tomb,
while you detain here, among us, something
that belongs to the gods who live below
our world—the naked unwept corpse you've robbed
of the solemn grieving we owe our dead.
None of this should have been any concern
of yours—or of the Olympian gods—
but you have involved them in your outrage!
Therefore, avengers wait to ambush you—   1190
the Furies sent by Hades and its gods
will punish you for the crimes I have named.

Do you think someone hired me to tell you this?
It won't be long before wailing breaks out
from the women and men in your own house.
And hatred against you will surge in all

the countries whose sons, in mangled pieces,
received their rites of burial
from dogs, wild beasts, or flapping birds
who have carried the stench of defilement   1200
to the homelands and the hearths of the dead.

Since you've provoked me, these are the arrows
I have shot in anger, like a bowman,
straight at your heart—arrows you cannot dodge,
and whose pain you will feel.
                              Lad, take me home—
let this man turn his anger on younger
people. That might teach him to hold his tongue,
and to think more wisely than he does now.

Exit TIRESIAS led by the Lad.

LEADER

This old man leaves stark prophecies behind.
Never once, while my hair has gone from black   1210
to white, has this prophet told Thebes a lie.

KREON

I'm well aware of that. It unnerves me.
Surrender would be devastating,
but if I stand firm, I could be destroyed.

LEADER

What you need is some very clear advice,
son of Menoikeus.

KREON

                What must I do?
If you have such advice, give it to me.

LEADER

Free the girl from her underground prison.
Build a tomb for the corpse you have let rot.

KREON

That's your advice? I should surrender?   1220

LEADER

Yes, King. Do it now. For the gods
act quickly to abort human folly.

KREON

I can hardly say this. But I'll give up
convictions I hold passionately—
and do what you ask. We can't fight
the raw power of destiny.

LEADER

                Then go!
Yourself. Delegate this to no one.

KREON

I'll go just as I am. Move out, men. Now!
All of you, bring axes and run toward
that rising ground. You can see it from here.   1230
Because I'm the one who has changed, I who

locked her away will go there to free her.
My heart is telling me we must obey
established law until the day we die.

Exit KREON and his Men toward open country.

ELDERS
God with myriad names—
lustrous child
of Kadmos' daughter,
son of thundering Zeus—
you govern fabled Italy,
you preside at Eleusis,   1240
secluded Valley of Demeter
that welcomes all pilgrims.
O Bakkhos! Thebes
is your homeland,
mother city of maenads
on the quietly flowing
Ismenos, where the dragon's
teeth were sown.

Now you stand on the ridges rising
up the twin peaks of Parnassos.   1250
There through the wavering
smoke-haze your torches flare.
There walk your devotees,
the nymphs of Korykia,
beside Kastalia's fountains.

Thick-woven ivy on Nysa's sloping hills,
grape-clusters ripe on verdant shorelines
propel you here, while voices
of more than human power
sing "Evohoi!"—your name divine—   1260
when the streets of Thebes
are your final destination.

By honoring Thebes
beyond all cities,
you honor your mother
whom the lightning killed.
Now a plague
ravages our city. Come home
on healing footsteps—down
the slopes of Parnassos,   1270
or over the howling channel.
Stars breathing their gentle fire
shine joy on you as they rise,
O master of nocturnal voices!
Take shape before our eyes, Bakkhos,
son of Zeus our king, let the Thyiads
come with you, let them climb
the mad heights of frenzy
as you, Iakkhos, the bountiful,
watch them   1280
dance through the night.

Enter MESSENGER.

MESSENGER

Neighbors, who live not far from the grand
old houses of Amphion and Kadmos,
you can't trust anything in a person's life—
praiseworthy or shameful—never to change.
Fate lifts up—and Fate cuts down—both the lucky
and the unlucky, day in and day out.
No prophet can tell us what happens next.
Kreon always seemed someone to envy,
to me at least. He saved from attack   1290
the homeland where we sons of Kadmos live.
This won him absolute power. He was
the brilliant father of patrician children.
Now it has all slipped away. For when things
that give pleasure and meaning to our lives
desert a man, he's not a human being
anymore—he becomes a breathing corpse.
Amass wealth if you can, show off your house.
Display the panache of a great monarch.
But if joy disappears from your life,   1300
I wouldn't give the shadow cast by smoke
for all you possess. Only happiness matters.

LEADER

Should our masters expect more grief? What's happened?

MESSENGER

Death. And the killer is alive.

LEADER

Name the murderer. Name the dead. Tell us.

MESSENGER

Haimon is dead. The hand that killed him was his own . . .

LEADER

. . . father's? Or do you mean he killed himself?

MESSENGER

He killed himself. Raging at his killer father.

LEADER

Tiresias, you spoke the truth.

MESSENGER

You know the facts. Now you must cope with them.   1310

Enter EURYDIKE.

LEADER

I see Eurydike, soon to be crushed,
approaching from inside the house.
She may have heard what's happened to her son.

EURYDIKE

I heard all of you speaking as I came out—
on my way to offer prayers to Athena.
I happened to unlatch the gate,

to open it, when words of our disaster
carried to my ears. I fainted, terrified
and dumbstruck, in the arms of my servant.
Please tell me your news. Tell me all of it.   1320
I'm someone who has lived through misfortune.

MESSENGER

O my dear Queen, I will spare you nothing.
I'll tell you truthfully what I've just seen.
Why should I say something to soothe you
that will later prove me a liar?
Straight talk is always best.
I traveled with your husband to the far
edge of the plain where Polyneikes' corpse,
mangled by wild dogs, lay still uncared for.

We prayed for mercy to the Goddess   1330
of Roadways, and to Pluto, asking them
to restrain their anger. We washed his remains
with purified water. Using boughs stripped
from nearby bushes, we burned what was left,
then mounded a tomb from his native earth.

After that we turned toward the girl's deadly
wedding cavern—with its bed of cold stone.
Still far off, we heard an enormous wail
coming from somewhere near the unhallowed
portico—so we turned back to tell Kreon.   1340
As the king arrived, these incoherent

despairing shouts echoed all around him.
First he groaned, then he yelled out in raw pain,

"Am I a prophet? Will my worst fears come true?
Am I walking down the bitterest street
of my life? That's my son's voice greeting me!

"Move quickly, men. Run through that narrow gap
where the stones have been pulled loose from the wall.
Go where the cavern opens out. Tell me
the truth—is that Haimon's voice I'm hearing,   1350
or have the gods played some trick on my ears?"

Following orders from our despondent
master, we stared in. At the tomb's far end
there she was, hanging by the neck, a noose
of finely woven linen holding her aloft.
Haimon fell against her, hugging her waist,
grieving for the bride he'd lost to Hades,
for his father's acts, for his own doomed love.

When Kreon saw all this he stepped inside,
groaned horribly, and called out to his son: 1360
"My desperate child! What have you done? What
did you think you were doing? When did the gods
destroy your reason? Come out of there, son.
I beg you."

       His son then glared straight at him
with savage eyes, spat in his face, spoke not

one word in answer, but drew his two-edged sword.
His father leapt back. Haimon missed his thrust.
Then this raging youth—with no warning—turned
on himself, tensed his body to the sword,
and drove half its length deep into his side.   1370
Still conscious, he clung to her with limp arms,
gasping for breath, spurts of his blood pulsing
onto her white cheek.

                Then he lay there, his dead
body embracing hers, married at last,
poor man—not up here, but somewhere
in Hades—proving that of all mankind's
evils, thoughtless violence is the worst.

Exit EURYDIKE.

LEADER

What do you make of that? She turns and leaves
without saying one word, brave or bitter.

MESSENGER

I don't like it. I hope that having heard   1380
the sorry way her son died, she won't grieve
for him in public. Maybe she's gone
to ask her maids to mourn him in the house.
This woman never loses her composure.

LEADER

I'm not so sure. To me this strange silence
seems ominous as an outburst of grief.

MESSENGER

I'll go in and find out.
She could have disguised the real
intent of her impassioned heart.
But I agree: her silence is alarming.   1390

Exit MESSENGER into the palace; KREON enters carrying the body of HAIMON
wrapped in cloth; his Men follow, bringing a bier on which KREON will lay his
son in due course.

LEADER

Here comes our king, burdened
with a message all too clear:
this wasn't caused by anyone's vengeance—
may I say it?—but by his own father's blunders.

KREON

Oh, what errors of the mind I have made!
Deadly, bullheaded blunders.
You all see it—the man
who murdered, and the son
who's dead. What I did
was blind and wrong!   1400
You died so young, my son.
Your death happened so fast!
Your life was cut short
not through your mad acts,
but through mine.

LEADER

You saw the right course of action
but took it far too late.

KREON

I've learned that lesson now—
in all its bitterness.
Sometime back, a god struck   1410
my head an immense blow,
it drove me
to act in brutal ways,
ways that stamped out
all my happiness.
What burdens and what pain
men suffer and endure.

Enter MESSENGER from the palace.

MESSENGER

Master, your hands are full of sorrow,
you bear its full weight.
But other sorrows are in store—   1420
you'll face them soon, inside your house.

KREON

Can any new
calamity make
what's happened worse?

MESSENGER

Your wife is dead—so much
a loving mother to your son,
poor woman, that she died
of wounds just now inflicted.

KREON

Oh Hades, you are hard
to appease! We flood   1430
your harbor. You want more.
Why are you trying
to destroy me?
(turning to MESSENGER)
What have you to tell me
this time?—you who bring
nothing but deadly news.
I was hardly alive, and now, my young friend,
you've come back to kill me again.
Son, what are you telling me?
What is this newest message   1440

—the palace doors open; EURYDIKE's corpse is revealed; KREON sighs—

that buries me? My wife is dead.
Slaughter after slaughter.

LEADER

Now you see it. Your house no longer hides it.

KREON

I see one more violent death. With what
else can Fate punish me? I have

just held my dead son in my arms—
now I see another dear body.
Ahhh. Unhappy mother, oh my son.

MESSENGER

There, at the altar, she pierced
herself with a sharp blade.   1450
Her eyes went quietly dark
and she closed them.
She had first mourned aloud
the empty marriage bed
of her dead son Megareus.
Then with her last breath
she cursed you, Kreon,
killer of your own son.

KREON

Ahhh! That sends fear
surging through me.   1460
Why hasn't someone
driven a two-edged
sword through my heart?
I'm a wretched coward,
awash with terror.

MESSENGER

The woman whose corpse you see
condemns you for the deaths of her sons.

KREON

Tell me how she did it.

MESSENGER

She drove the blade below her liver,
so she could suffer the same wound   1470
that killed Haimon, for whom she mourns.

KREON

There's no one I can blame,
no other mortal.
I am the only one.

*KREON looks at and touches the body of HAIMON as his Men assemble to
escort him offstage.*

I killed you, that's the reality.
Men, take me inside.
I'm less than nothing now.

LEADER

You are doing what's right,
if any right can be found
among all these misfortunes.   1480
Better to say little
in the face of evil.

KREON

Let it come, let it happen now—
let my own kindest fate

make this my final day on earth.
That would be kindness itself.
Let it happen, let it come.
Never let me see
tomorrow's dawn.

LEADER

That's in the future. We   1490
must deal with the present.
The future will be shaped
by those who control it.

KREON

My deepest desires are in that prayer.

LEADER

Stop your prayers.
No human being
evades calamity
once it has struck.

KREON puts his hand on HAIMON's corpse.

KREON

Take me from this place.
A foolish, impulsive man   1500
who killed you, my son, mindlessly,
killed you as well, my wife.
I'm truly cursed! I don't know

where to rest my eyes,
or on whose shoulders
I can lean my weight.
My hands warp
all they touch.

*KREON, still touching HAIMON's corpse, looks toward EURYDIKE's, then lifts
his hand and moves off toward the palace.*

And over there,
Fate's avalanche   1510
pounds my head.

LEADER
Good sense is crucial
to human happiness.
Never fail to respect the gods,
for the huge claims of proud men
are always hugely punished—
by blows that, as the proud grow old,
pound wisdom through their minds.

ALL leave.

NOTES TO THE PLAY

Scene Antigone's awareness of Kreon's decree and Polyneikes' unburied corpse suggests that she had left the palace to visit the city (and perhaps the battlefield). If so, she would enter from outside the palace gates.

1–2 *Born . . . womb* The Greek word *autadelphon*, translated with *koinon* (kindred) as a single phrase "born like me from that same womb," literally means "selfsame womb." *Koinon*, subsumed into the phrase as "like me," may also be rendered as "kindred" (Jebb) or "linked to me" (Lloyd-Jones). Antigone's first words to Ismene thus strike a chord that reverberates throughout the drama: their shared family inheritance includes horrific misfortunes that go back to their conceptions and births. The Greek word *kara* is translated with the endearment "love." Tyrrell and Bennett write, "Sophocles' avoidance of a usual word for sister may also point to Ismene as less important to Antigone in that capacity than as a 'wombmate' . . . and also suggests the excessive closeness brought about by Oedipus, their common father and brother" (31).

5–8 *our lives . . . you and I haven't seen and shared* Antigone speaks of her sister and herself as united by common interests, as well as blood, until 94. After Ismene refuses to help bury Polyneikes (95–96), Antigone stops referring to herself and Ismene as a pair.

9 *new command* Kreon, the girls' uncle, Thebes' military leader, or *strategos*, and now its new king, presumably declared this edict only hours earlier, as soon as the Argive army's retreat was apparent.

15 *as if they were our enemies!* This suggests that the bodies of all the dead Argive attackers have been left unburied. We later learn from Tiresias that this is indeed the case. Polyneikes fits both the category of *philos*, loved one or family member, and that of *ekthros*, enemy.

20 *the double blow* After Oedipus departed Thebes in exile to Athens, his sons Eteokles and Polyneikes agreed to alternate as king. But Eteokles refused to step down at the end of his year and banished his brother. Polyneikes moved to Argos, married King Adrastos' daughter, and solicited support for a campaign to regain power in his home city. He and six other Argive captains attacked the seven gates of Thebes. During the battle, the brothers apparently struck each other with simultaneous deadly spear thrusts, a mode of death that fulfilled the curse against his sons delivered by Oedipus in the *Kolonos*. (Aspects of this war are the subject of Aeschylus' *Seven Against Thebes* and Euripides' *Phoenician Women* and *The Suppliants*.)

24 *past the gates* Refers to the house gates, not the outer palace gates that lead to the town.

32 *The dead will respect him* According to fifth-century Greek religious belief, failure to mound earth over a dead family member and perform the required funeral rituals would

cause those already dead in Hades to shun and scorn such a dishonored shade (ghost) when it arrived among them.

43 *stoned to death* Since communal stoning by many citizens would have been an appropriate method of execution for Polyneikes, a traitor to his own people, a citizen who defied the city to bury a traitor would be fittingly sentenced to the same method of execution.

48–49 *yanking the knot . . . pry it loose* The image comes from weaving, strictly a woman's occupation for the Greeks. Ismene might be sarcastically asking her sister how her weaving skills could be of any use in burying Polyneikes and confronting Kreon.

52 *lift his body* To cover Polyneikes' heavy body with the substantial mounding of earth that Antigone envisions at 97–98, she will need Ismene's help. Without that help she would be forced to perform a more limited ceremony—a dusting with earth, a poured libation, screams of grief—such as the Guard will soon describe.

58–70 *our father's / destruction . . . kin murder!* Ismene recalls the gods' savage punishment of their parents to highlight the difference between Oedipus' and Jokasta's "horrible deeds" and the lesser matter of a failed ritual, which she hopes the gods and the dead ("the Spirits," 78) will understand and forgive.

71–72 *how much worse / our own deaths* Ismene imagines the threatened stoning as a much harsher method of death than their mother's hanging, but "much worse" could also refer to the fact that there are no women left in the family to perform the sacred burial rituals mentioned in the note to

52—rituals that only women could perform. See *Antigone* introduction, pp. 3–4.

87–88 *lie down / next to* The Greek word Antigone uses here for lying down, *keisomai*, would be equally appropriate to describe lying in death (either before burial or in Hades) or having sexual relations with a lover (Blundell 1989, 110). The words used to describe their kinship, *philê* with *philou*, (translated here as "I who love him" next to "him who loves me") accentuate both the emotional bond and the physical proximity of the bodies (Griffith, 135).

89 *criminal conduct* The Greek words *hosia panourgesas* (literally, "sacred transgressions") refer primarily to the outlawed act of burying her "traitor" brother, but they also allude, given the way they are embedded in the sentence, to the incestuous love Antigone might feel for Polyneikes.

107 *those who matter* Most likely the gods; perhaps also Polyneikes. See 487–508, an elaboration of Antigone's intention to please Hades and the gods of the underworld.

Exit ANTIGONE She leaves abruptly to look for Polyneikes' body on the battlefield, ignoring Ismene's warning and concern.

121–122 *Morning sunlight . . . on seven-gated Thebes!* The Elders begin a song that celebrates Thebes' victory over Argos. Notably missing from the song is any reference to what preoccupies Kreon: punishing the dead body of Polyneikes. Joy and celebration, gratitude to Dionysos, Ares, and all the other gods, are paramount.

124 *Dirke* One of two rivers flowing through Thebes. The other is the Ismenos.

127 *white shield* The name of the region from which the attacking army comes, Argos, suggests silvery or shining whiteness.

128 *sharp piercing bit* The Argive army is portrayed as a wild vicious horse and the defending Thebans as the horse tamer who subdues it—by using a particularly nasty bit that digs into the horse's jaw.

131 *quarrelsome* A pun, since Polyneikes' name means literally "serial battler."

133 *white-feathered Eagle* An emblem of Argos.

141–142 *Firegod's / incendiary pine tar* Literally, "Hephestos' pine-fed flame." Balls of pine pitch were set afire and lobbed via catapult over defensive walls and onto wooden houses in besieged cities.

146 *Dragon* The ancestral "snake" with whom Thebans identified. See *Oedipus the King*, note to 96.

148 *Zeus hates a proud tongue* A reference to Kapaneus. See *Kolonos*, note to 1441.

169–170 *trophies / for Zeus* At the end of a battle, the armor of the defeated troops was collected and fastened to totem-like structures in honor of Zeus.

174 *Victory* The wingèd goddess Niké.

181 *each god's temple* With the fighting over and victory secured, every god who might have played a part in helping Thebes win must be honored in his or her own temple, hence the festive midnight rounds.

183–184 *Bakkhos, the god whose dancing / rocks Thebes*
Bakkhos, an alternate name for Dionysos, is characteristi-
cally worshipped by song and a drum-accompanied dance.
He often makes his presence felt by causing an earthquake.
See *Oedipus the King*, note to 250.

185–191 *our new king . . . Council of the Wise* This will be
Kreon's first consultation with this body of seasoned politi-
cians since his assumption of power the previous day. It will
turn out that he neither solicits nor welcomes their opin-
ions.

204 *defiled by his own brother's blood* Kin murder had been
for centuries an intensely feared crime, since it inflicted in-
famy and uncleanness on the guilty; such defilement was dif-
ficult to cleanse. In this case, it will be impossible because
the guilty brothers are both dead.

207–212 *character, / policies . . . sound advice* By setting stan-
dards according to which a ruler should be judged, Kreon
focuses attention on his coming failures and blunders as a
leader.

222–223 *It's only on board . . . true friends* Kreon's assess-
ment of friendship, for him defined in the context of loy-
alty to one's city, differs startlingly from Antigone's. She
believes that friends are made only at birth, an indication
of her strong ties to family. The Greek word used in both
of their assessments of "friendship" is *philia*. See note to
567–568.

239 *ugly . . . disgrace* The practice of refusing burial to dead
enemies was a contentious political issue in fifth-century
Greece that was dramatized in two other surviving plays,

The Suppliants of Aeschylus and *The Suppliant Women* of Euripides.

266 *talking annihilation* I follow here Griffith's interpretation of the Greek line 234 and his suggestion that a translation of the phrase *to medon exerô* should express the Guard's fear that his story might turn him into "nothing"—i.e., get him killed.

279–280 *thirsty / dust . . . rituals* Polyneikes' body was not buried or entombed as would have been customary, but appears to have received a minimal ritual from a source unknown. See note to 310.

310 *inspired by the gods?* The mysterious circumstances of the burial described by the Guard—no tracks, no footprints— suggest to the Leader that the gods have either performed or otherwise prompted the minimal burial of Polyneikes. If so, punishing a human agent would be dangerously offensive to the gods who have intervened on Polyneikes' behalf.

340 *strung up—and you'll hang* Kreon, with characteristic bluster, threatens to torture and kill anyone within earshot who refuses to track down and hand over the person who buried Polyneikes.

352 *since you were born* Implies that the Guard is a household servant or slave with whom Kreon has been long acquainted.

364–365 *Wonders abound . . . astounding than man!* Literally, "There are many wonders / terrors but none as wonderful / terrible as man." The Greek word *ta deina* can mean either "wonderful" or "terrible." Most scholars and translators stress both the positive and negative capacities of humans in the context of this ode (364–413). I omit the "terrifying" dimension in 364 because, on inspection, virtually all the examples of humankind's activity in the ode contributed to the development of civilization. But my choice of the word "astounding" in 365 alludes to the human capacity for evil. At the end of the ode, when humankind's "terrifying" or destructive aspect does surface, the Elders condemn it. The city's banishment of an isolated "reckless and corrupt" over-reacher reflects the Elders' final judgment.

373 *stallion-sired mules* Literally, "the children of horses." Mules were the preferred draft animals used on Greek farms.

404–405 *follow the laws / Earth teaches him* With these lines, Sophocles reminds us that Kreon and Antigone not only differ about which laws and which gods to obey, but that they understand "earth" in very different terms: "for Kreon, earth is the political territory of Thebes, defined by human law; for Antigone, it is the realm of the gods below, who protect the rites of the dead" (Segal 2003, 130–131).

463–464 *piercing scream . . . nest robbed* Grieving women were often compared to mother birds robbed of their nestlings. But here Sophocles' simile suggests that Antigone is, in the traditional Greek sense, a bird as omen, thus a vehicle for delivering the gods' will. Images of Polyneikes' corpse, exposed as human carrion, intensify the significance. Other readings are equally pertinent and foreboding: the empty nest recalls the children who might have been born to Antigone and Haimon; Polyneikes' empty grave, the result of battle and marriage to King Adrastos' daughter Argeia (see note to 954–955); and the empty nest of Kreon after the suicide of his son and wife. See Tyrrell and Bennett,

66–67. (Also cf. Sophocles' use of the metaphor in *Oedipus the King* [62] when the Priest calls Oedipus "a bird from god.")

469 *three cool swallows* As a part of funeral ritual, ancient Greeks poured libations directly onto the grave for a dead relative to drink.

471–473 *charged her . . . now this one. / Didn't deny a thing* Sophoclean scholars have long debated whether Antigone performed only the second or both "burials" of Polyneikes, especially since the first burial, according to the Guard, seems to have been performed by a being who left no evidence behind, and might well be a divine or other airborne creature. Here Antigone accepts blame for both burials. The difficulties in believing Antigone was the first duster of the body, however, are considerable: how did she do it without leaving a trace? The gods were entirely capable of intervening to *protect* Polyneikes' body from animals until it could be given a proper honoring. (In Homer's *Iliad* gods protected both Sarpedon and Hector.) What the gods cannot do is perform full burial rites, which are the responsibility of blood kin alone. For a most interesting and persuasive discussion of this issue, see Tyrrell and Bennett (54–62).

492 *unwritten and infallible laws* Such laws were a part of both legal and religious thought. Examples of unwritten laws include the imperative to bury the dead according to precise ancient customs, the prohibition against killing blood kin, and the permanent defilement of kin-slayers.

509–510 *girl's nature . . . her father's* In both his Theban and Athenian incarnations (in *Oedipus the King* and the *Kolonos*), Sophocles' character Oedipus displays a reckless and hasty violence in thought and action that the Leader now finds in Antigone. Antigone's "savage" (or *oumós*, "raw") nature primarily attacks Kreon and the politics he represents, and Ismene for her refusal to help perform Polyneikes' burial rituals. Griffith notes that *oumós* "is a very strong term to apply to anyone, esp. a young woman (elsewhere in tragedy used only of men)" (204). Segal notes that the word is reserved for the worst crimes and especially strong taboos pertaining to family (1981, 34). It might therefore be interpreted to include her incestuous feeling for Polyneikes implied at 87–88.

531 *screaming, hysterical, deranged* Ismene's fit could be the result of fear for Antigone's recklessness or of distress at her own refusal to help her sister bury Polyneikes. It is surely not what Kreon assumes: a fit of guilt as she contemplates treachery.

550 *bite their tongues* The verb Antigone uses here, *upillousin*, which I translate as "bite," refers to the way in which a cowering dog clamps its tail between its legs.

563 *Hades . . . rituals* Antigone insists Hades makes no distinctions or exceptions among the dead. He demands they all be honored and buried.

567–568 *I made no enemies . . . friends* Traditionally this line has been translated as Jebb has it: "'Tis not my nature to join in hating, only in loving" (1888, 102). But Lloyd-Jones and Wilson state that *physis*, which Jebb translates as "nature," must refer in this context to "one's birth." They argue that the Greeks believed one can make *friends* by birth, but never *enemies* (1990, 126). So translated in this context, the line makes clearer sense of Antigone's conduct in the drama, since the Greeks' sense of "hating," and certainly our own, is evident throughout in Antigone's temperament and her words. Lloyd-Jones and Wilson's solution spares scholars many an interpretive contortion. Those producing the play who believe Antigone is referring to her loving nature might substitute: "It's my nature to share love, not hatred."

594 *sprang to his defense* At 56 Ismene admitted she was afraid of betraying Kreon, and at 95–96 she declared her refusal to defy the city.

602 *Some think you're right* Those who agree with Ismene are living, principally Kreon; those who agree with Antigone, her dead family and the underworld gods, are in Hades.

603 *equally wrong* They can't be equally wrong—at least in the gods' eyes: Hades' demand that kin be buried is confirmed in the resolution of the drama.

615 *field to plow* The metaphor of a woman's body as a field or furrow for plowing, common in ancient Greece, echoes Athenian marriage contracts (Blundell 1989, 120). Athenian audiences would not have normally found Kreon's use of it offensive, but his insensitivity to both Antigone and Haimon could have struck them as obscene (Tyrrell and Bennett, 78–79).

628–691 *Lucky are those . . . catastrophe* The particular evil the Elders have in mind in this ode is peculiar to families, and it cannot be evaded or defeated by any action or virtue of a family member. The ray of hope suggested by Antigone's character and vigor as "the last rootstock" is snuffed out by her insistence on burying her brother and by Kreon's "reckless talk" and mental "Furies," but the failure of a generation to "protect its own youth" also applies to Kreon and

Haimon as well. The ode offers a more general theory of human futility in its latter section: the gods punish humankind for achievement itself, and though hope sometimes is justified, it's usually delusive and deadly. Also, the foolish can't distinguish evil from noble motives; catastrophe results. If Kreon (onstage in the background) hears this ode, he seems unaware that it targets him.

644 *Labdakids* Oedipus' ancestral family.

657 *blood-drenched dust* The image recalls the latest act committed by a member of the doomed House of Labdakos—Antigone's sprinkling of dust over Polyneikes. But it also evokes the brothers' dead bodies on the battlefield and, perhaps, the dust storm that swirled when Antigone performed the burial rites.

658 *death gods* Hades, Acheron, Persephone, Hermes.

660 *Furies in the mind* The goddesses called Furies—also referred to as the Erinys—typically punish the conscience for crimes committed against the family, especially kin murder, and they are often credited with unbalancing a person's judgment. The Furies first "appear" in ancient tragedy (in Aeschylus' *Libation Bearers*) to punish Orestes for killing his mother. Although the audience realizes that the goddesses have manifested themselves in Orestes' mind, none of the other characters onstage is aware of their presence. For more on their role in *Kolonos*, where they preside in their more benevolent incarnation as the Eumenides, see notes to 44–50 and 92 in that play.

670 *Olympos* The mountain, visible from ancient Thebes, was the home base of the Olympian gods, from Zeus through Hephestos.

686–691 *"Evil seems noble . . . hold off catastrophe"* These words of wisdom refer to the ancient Greeks' belief that the gods "destroy the judgment of a person bent on evil and destruction. As we might phrase it in our more psychologizing terms, the gods collaborate with the evil tendencies of the prospective criminal to lead him to his ruin" (Segal 2003, 140–141).

693 *youngest of your sons* Haimon has an older brother, Megareus. See note to 1095.

721 *turn ice-cold in your arms* Here Kreon's words foreshadow how Haimon will wrap his arms around Antigone not long after she commits suicide, at 1371. Sophocles intensifies the irony with Kreon's avowal at 699–700 that "we'll soon have an answer" as to whether Haimon will defend his bride or support Kreon's sentencing her to death—an answer that is "better than any prophet's."

730–731 *Zeus / of family life* Zeus Herkeios, literally, Zeus of the Fence (*herkos*), is a manifestation of Zeus who protects an extended family's welfare. He was worshipped within the boundaries of the house, usually at an inner courtyard shrine. Kreon implies that this "household" Zeus would disapprove of Antigone's burial of Polyneikes (and her invocation of kinship law as the motive behind it), since the god would not approve a family member's rebellion against the head of its household.

756 *sapped my wits* The Leader alludes ironically to Kreon's earlier insult at 312, where he accused the Leader of sounding old and senile.

785 *open him up* Haimon compares his father to a clay writing tablet that opened and closed like a book or laptop computer. Kreon, says his son, has nothing inside him.

828 *You will not marry her while she's* on *this earth* Another example of the irony in Kreon's "prophetic" powers. The "marriage" of Haimon and Antigone will indeed take place after her death. See 1373–1375.

855–856 *enough food to evade / defilement* The city would be defiled if Antigone, Kreon's blood relative, were executed at his command. By leaving enough food to sustain her for a while, Kreon might hope that she'll commit suicide in despair, as indeed she will, and thus relieve Thebes of defilement. But Kreon was wrong to think his conduct could elude the defilement that will harm all Thebes. See Tiresias' denunciation of Kreon at 1176–1208.

857 *pray there to Hades* Since Hades is Antigone's favored deity, he would logically be the one she turns to in a desperate situation. But Hades has no reputation for saving lives. By saying "Maybe he will spare her" Kreon sneers at Antigone's self-delusion.

861–880 *Love, you win . . . our lives* The Elders sing a brief celebration of Aphrodite and her son Eros, gods of Love—the emotion that Kreon leaves out of his calculations. He may remain onstage to hear the Elders enumerate Love's power over humans and beasts, and to hear them give Love its rightful place among the ancient powers and laws, written or unwritten. The ode presents a double paradox: The allure of the bride is both irresistible and destructive, as Antigone's allure for Haimon will prove to be. And what humans consider to be disastrous, the gods of Love deem as play or even mockery. (See Griffith, 260.)

863 *havoc with our herds* A literal translation. The word translated as "herds," *ktemasi*, can also refer to what the herds represent economically: wealth. The line could mean something like "love who . . . impoverishes us." I interpret it with Griffith (257) to mean that erotic power also drives animals into frenzy.

872–873 *wrench men's minds . . . off course* The image is of a chariot overturning on a race course. Love at the intensity the Elders register here made even the ancients unsafe drivers.

dressed in purple as a bride Throughout her final scene, Antigone conducts herself as if she were preparing for her wedding. Her spoken and sung speeches are dense with allusions, both ironic and plaintive, to a bride's expectations. Having her appear in a traditional Greek purple bridal costume would visually reinforce Sophocles' verbal imagery. Indeed, wedding and funeral rituals were deeply associative of each other in Athenian culture; they both signified a similar transition in life. Upon leaving her father's house, the bride entered the house of another man and perished as a virgin; the dead entered Hades' house, never to return (Tyrrell and Bennett, 98). Sophocles' audience would have been attuned to the visual and verbal clues that connected the rituals of marriage and death.

891 *Acheron* The river god of a stream that flows through Hades.

895 *River of Pain* A literal rendering of the meaning of Acheron.

901 *enter Hades . . . still alive* A bit of sophistry on the Elders' part. Antigone will be imprisoned below ground, thus in proximity to Hades, and she will still be alive. But only the truly dead ever enter the real place. The Elders probably want to emphasize Antigone's exercise of free choice in committing the act that led to her death sentence.

903–905 *Phrygian stranger . . . Mount Sipylos* The Phyrigian stranger, or Niobe, was the daughter of King Tantalos of Lydia. She married Amphion, a king of Thebes, and bore him an equal number of sons and daughters (six of each, according to Homer; other versions of the myth say seven, nine, or ten). After Niobe boasted that she was superior to the goddess Leto, who had only one of each, Leto sent her children, who just happened to be Apollo and Artemis, to kill Niobe's. Niobe wept for nine days and nights, after which the Olympian gods turned her to a stone face embedded on a cliff on Mount Sipylos (where her father lived). The rain and snow eternally dripping from this stone image were seen as tears. In other versions of the myth, Niobe is a mortal whose boast of being superior to a divinity provoked her punishment. Sophocles' audience would have recognized his artistic license in making her a god. Tyrrell and Bennett suggest that Sophocles' purpose was to accentuate Antigone's own likening of herself to a god, considered by fifth-century Greeks as "boastfulness beyond the pale" (107). Sophocles also could have intended to soften the Leader's reproach at 914–919, where he calls her godlike fate "no small honor."

906 *Living rock* In Niobe's case, the metaphor of a body turned to stone alludes to the end of her fertility; in Antigone's case, the allusion is first to her never-to-be-penetrated virgin

body. Seaford interprets the stone in both cases as enclosing them with their natal families (Seaford 1994, 351).

932 *heaped-up rock-bound prison* Suggests that Antigone's "tomb" was not a geologically formed cave but man-made, with earth piled above a hollowed lower chamber.

933 *without a friend* Antigone may have admirers in Thebes (as Haimon insists), but none comes forward to grieve for her, presumably out of fear. And of course Antigone no longer considers her sister Ismene to be a *philê*, or family member, thus she is not a possible mourner.

943–956 *You've touched . . . so was I* In this lyric, Antigone traces her family curse not to Laios' original disobedience of Apollo, but to her mother's incest. (The focus on her mother's responsibility echoes her opening words to Ismene, "born . . . from that same womb.") As Segal notes, "kinship as a function of female procreative power [was] embedded in Greek culture" (1998, 183). Throughout this meditation, Antigone sees marriage as a maker of defilement and death, not of children and life (see note to 954–955 and the counterpart to her speech, Oedipus' howl of pain against marriages in *Oedipus the King*, 1591–1596).

954–955 *deadly / marriage* By marrying Argeia, the daughter of the Argive king Adrastos, Polyneikes gained the military support he needed to attack Thebes; thus his marriage contributed to his death in battle.

980 *pure as far as she's concerned* Kreon assumes his precautions—leaving her a small ration of food and enclosing her in a tomb away from the city—will be enough to evade the defilement of kin murder.

983–984 *My tomb ... dug from rock* The tomb has three
    identities for Antigone: it is the grave Kreon sentenced her
    to in punishment for attempting to violate his decree; it is
    the nuptial bedroom in which she will wed Hades; and it is the
    hollow in which she will dwell with her parents and dead
    brothers (Tyrrell and Bennett, 111).

996–1013 *I honored you ... hollow tomb* The authenticity of
    these lines has been questioned at least since Goethe (in 1827)
    famously expressed the hope that some classical scholar would
    prove them spurious. Though many editors and critics have
    impugned the lines, including Jebb and Winnington-Ingram,
    confidence in their genuineness has grown in recent years. On
    the one hand, Lloyd-Jones and Wilson (1990 and 1997) cor-
    rectly state that objections to them are invariably subjective.
    On the other hand, contemporary scholars, e.g., Tyrrell and
    Bennett, and Griffith, have argued that their content conforms
    to Antigone's understanding of both herself and the duties to
    kin as prescribed by divine law. For those producing the play
    and unconvinced of their authenticity, or who believe includ-
    ing them would divert audience attention into seemingly arid
    and arcane matters, these lines can be omitted en bloc with-
    out disrupting the flow and logic of the remaining lines.

1009 *he pulls me by the wrist* After the wedding feast, the bride
    was traditionally pulled by the wrist (from a table with other
    women) in a symbolic act of abduction and led away by the
    bridegroom. Although Antigone imagines Hades as her bride-
    groom, she seems here to allude to Kreon as the person who
    prevents her from a marriage on earth. Kreon does not actually
    lead Antigone away himself but delegates the act to his men.

1021–1022 *I want them / to suffer the pain* Antigone's call for vengeance might be directed at the citizens of Thebes who did not defend her and her cause, but Kreon is her primary target. Not having any *philoi* left to mourn her or to take vengeance on Kreon, she must depend on the gods, she thinks, and she appeals to them directly.

1032 *Look at me, princely citizens* In the moments before she gives herself to Hades, Antigone enacts her own version of *anakalyptêria*, the bride's traditional lifting of her veil for the first time among men. The penetration of the men's eyes was symbolic of her imminent loss of virginity. The gesture of showing her face, as made by a Greek bride whose passivity was taken for granted, was a speechless invitation. But here Antigone acts aggressively, as she did in performing burial rituals for Polyneikes, and calls out to the Elders.

1036 *Danaë* Danaë's father, Akrisios, king of Argos, locked her in a bronze tower because an oracle prophesied that a son of hers would someday kill him. Zeus impregnated her with a shower of gold, and she gave birth to Perseus, who did in fact kill Akrisios accidentally while throwing a discus. Two other mythological characters in this ode were in some way imprisoned; see notes to 1051 and 1081–1084.

1051 *Lycurgos* According to Homer's *Iliad* (6.130ff.) Lycurgos attacked Dionysos, forcing the young god and his nurses to take refuge in the sea. Soon after Dionysos retaliated by blinding him, Lycurgos died. Sophocles likely knew other versions of the myth, and seems to draw here on the versions of Apollodorus (I. 35) and Hyginus (*Fab.* 132), in which Dionysos drives Lycurgos mad.

1066–1068 *Black Rocks . . . Bosphoros' channel* The Bosphoros, a narrow strait that joined the Black Sea with the Sea of Marmara and the Mediterranean, divided Asia and Europe; the Black Rocks, over which a swift current passed, have been worn away over the past 2,400 years.

1071 *Ares* The god of cruel bloodshed, considered to be of Thracian origin, was unpopular in the ancient world, and important only in Thebes and perhaps Athens. In mythology he is nearly always portrayed as an instigator of violence or a tempestuous lover; he never develops a moral function, as do Zeus, Apollo, and Dionysos, on his own terms, as the people's god.

1073 *savage wife of Phineus* When Phineus, a Thracian king, cast off his wife Kleopatra—who was the daughter of Boreas, the North Wind—he married Eidothea, who blinded Phineus' two sons (for reasons unclear in the various versions of the myth).

1081–1084 *a woman unhappy . . . Erektheids* The unhappy woman, distraught because her marriage ended, is Kleopatra, the mother of Phineus' blinded sons. Her mother was Oreithyia, daughter of Erektheus, a king of Athens. Sophocles supposed Kleopatra's story to be familiar to his audience—although he doesn't mention it here, she was imprisoned by Phineas—and clearly means to connect her fate to Antigone's (Jebb 1888, 966n).

TIRESIAS . . . Lad Thebes' resident prophet, always accompanied by a young boy, also appears at critical moments in *Oedipus the King* and Euripides' *Bakkhai.*

1095 *questioned the advice* This may be a reference to advice Tiresias had given within the last few days concerning how best to divinely protect Thebes against the Argive onslaught (see note to 20). In one version of the myth of the Seven Against Thebes, Tiresias advises Kreon to sacrifice his eldest son, Megareus, mentioned at 1455, in order for Thebes to prevail.

1096 *straight course* Tiresias' use of "straight," or *orthos*, echoes Kreon's repeated use of the word in various forms to characterize his statesmanlike virtues of being upright and on course. His obsession with "straightness" carries over to manipulating people as expertly as one might steer a ship.

1106–1107 *They screeched . . . was drowned out* Birds were a major medium of communication between gods and mortals. Because the birds' angry screeching has made their songs unintelligible, Tiresias interprets the screeching itself as a sign of the gods' extreme displeasure with Kreon's recent acts and decrees. See note to 463–464.

1111 *sacrificial fire* Tiresias burns a large animal in the god's honor in order to regain his good will. Hephestos, god of fire, snuffs it out, thus blocking the gesture. At this point, Tiresias' prophetic drill shifts to examining the inner organs of the animal for useful omens.

1113–1117 *charred thighbones . . . fat enfolding them* Tiresias recounts how the sacrifice failed. The offering, probably the meat of an ox, should have gone up in flames when it was ignited—the fragrant smoke ascending like a prayer to the gods above. Instead, the fire smoldered, fat oozed into the ashes, and the gallbladder burst its stench into the air. The "vivid and repulsive description . . . [suggests] the putrescent corpse of Polyneikes" (Griffith, 299).

1117–1118 *attempt / at prophecy failed* Neither the animal's organs nor the sacrifice seeking divine advice yields any readable communications from the gods. Tiresias instead gives Kreon sensible advice of his own, unsanctioned by Apollo.

1122–1123 *city's altars . . . defiled* Because neither Polyneikes nor the Argive soldiers were properly mourned and buried, their dishonored flesh, spread throughout the city by dogs and birds, defiles Thebes.

1129–1130 *keen cries . . . garbled / by . . . thickened blood* Tiresias makes a direct connection between the city's defilement and the gods' displeasure at the city's leader.

1149 *silver from Sardis* Literally, silver-gold (an alloy).

1155 *men can defile gods* Kreon distorts Tiresias' explanation of his wrongdoing. The point is not whether men defile gods, but that Thebans and Kreon have defiled themselves.

1191 *Furies sent by Hades* Presumably the Eumenides, who will punish Kreon for his impiety by attacking his family. See *Kolonos*, notes to 44–50.

1227 *Delegate this to no one* The Leader might be alluding to the fact that Kreon, after boasting that he'd lead Antigone to her tomb himself, assigned his soldiers to the task.

1231–1232 *I who / locked her away will . . . free her* At 1218–1219, the Leader advised Kreon to free Antigone from her tomb and then to bury Polyneikes. Kreon makes tending to Polyneikes' body his first priority. Though going first to Antigone might not have saved her life, Kreon's mindless reversal of the logical priority further damns him.

1235–1281 *God with myriad names . . . night* Just before the worst calamity occurs (or is announced) in each of the three Oedipus plays, the Chorus members sing their appeal for help to Dionysos. This ode presents a vivid picture of the orgiastic worship of the god on Parnassos, a mountain northeast of Delphi that was traditionally sacred to Apollo and the muses. In the winter months, Apollo ceded his shrine at Delphi to Dionysos and his cult; a festival was held every two years and attended by a sanctioned band of maenads. (See Guthrie, 178, 202.)

1237 *Kadmos' daughter* Semele. See *Kolonos*, notes to 741–743.

1240–1241 *Eleusis . . . Demeter* See *Kolonos*, notes to 749–750 and 1149–1154.

1254–1255 *nymphs of Korykia . . . Kastalia's fountains* Nymphs, young female spirits representing the divine powers of nature, were named specifically for their function or the locale in which they resided. Korykia, a stalactite cavern in Mount Parnassos, was an ancient place of sacrifice. The Kastalia is a stream that flows from the fissure of a high cliff in the mountain.

1256 *Nysa's sloping hills* The mountain where Dionysos was born in some versions of myth. See *Kolonos*, notes to 741–743.

1260 *Evohoi!* A shout made by Dionysos' worshippers to signal that the god was among them.

1265–1266 *mother / whom the lightning killed* Semele.

1271 *howling channel* The windy straits between the Greek mainland and the island of Euboea.

1276 *Thyiads* A troop of Attic women sent to join the revels of their Delphic sisters in the winter worship of Dionysos.

1279 *Iakkhos* A secondary cult name of Bakkhos or Dionysos.

Messenger From his demeanor, he is an educated and trusted palace servant.

1283 *Amphion and Kadmos* Early kings of Thebes.

Eurydike Kreon's wife. Within days, she has seen both her sons die as a result of choices made by her husband. Her name means "wide" (*eury*) "justice/penalty/satisfaction" (*dike*), which she will fittingly exact from Kreon by leaving him without a female family member to mourn his son (or, when he dies, himself).

1321 *lived through misfortune* This could be a reference to the (possibly) sacrificial murder of her son, Megareus, as well as to the events of Oedipus' reign. See note to 1095.

1330–1331 *Goddess / of Roadways . . . Pluto* The goddess Hekate was worshipped at crossroads in the form of a statue with three heads or three bodies. Her mention brings to mind the crossroads where Oedipus killed Laios (see *Oedipus the King*, 832). Pluto is another name for Hades.

1344 *Am I a prophet?* Kreon has unwittingly predicted the tragic outcome of his son's relationship to Antigone. See note to 721.

1354–1357 *hanging . . . he'd lost to Hades* The image of Haimon embracing Antigone around the waist as she hangs from a noose of linen (perhaps made from the veil she lifted in her bridal procession) evokes another Attic wedding ritual that has been depicted in vase paintings. After the groom leads the bride by the wrist from the feast, he lifts her bolt upright into the mule cart that will carry the couple to their nuptial bed. The groom demonstrates his physical strength and dominance over the bride; the bride submits in compliance and dignity by remaining rigidly in the posture (Tyrrell and Bennett, 142).

1365 *spat in his face* Literally, *ptúsas prosopoi*. This gesture reminds
    us of the crude advice Kreon gave his son at 723–724: "spit this girl
    out like the enemy she is"; in the Greek, *ptúsas osei te dusmene*.
    Sophoclean irony shows Kreon once again as a man whose arro-
    gant behavior comes back to haunt him. The metaphorical usage
    of 723–724 is not found elsewhere in tragedy but is common in
    epic and lyric; for this reason, and perhaps because genteel Vic-
    torian scholars refrained from translating literally such an un-
    gentlemanly act as spitting, Jebb and others of his era focus on
    the loathing and contempt implicit in the passages. (See Griffith,
    236, 338.)

1366 *two-edged* Literally, *diplos*, or "double." The blade kills
    Haimon the son and Haimon the potential father. See *Oedi-
    pus the King*, note to 1415.

1371–1374 *he clung to her . . . married at last* The "marriage"
    is consummated with *oxeian*, literally, "spurts," of Haimon's
    blood, not Antigone's.

1425–1426 *so much / a loving mother to your son* Literally, "the
    pammêtôr of the corpse," or, in the scholiast's understand-
    ing, "the mother in all respects." *Pammêtôr* connotes the great
    Mother Earth, Gaia, the true mother of all things. Gaia repeat-
    edly defends her offspring throughout the formative period of
    the universe against male aggressors who attempt to control her
    children or usurp her procreativity. Sophocles' use of the term
    here draws on Panhellenic myth in which the goddess unleashes
    her vengeance as a subordinate of Zeus. Eurydike's violent sui-
    cide presents Kreon with the silenced woman he wanted in An-
    tigone, and it gives Antigone the vengeance she sought against
    Kreon—a silent funeral (Tyrrell and Bennett, 149–51).

1430–1431 *we flood / your harbor* The dead arrive in Hades'
realm by a boat that transports them across the River Styx.
Kreon imagines his own dead family as a sacrifice made to
Hades, but one that fails to win the gods' goodwill.

WORKS CITED AND CONSULTED

Aeschylus. *The Complete Greek Tragedies*. Trans. Richmond Lattimore, ed. David Grene and Richmond Lattimore. Chicago: University of Chicago Press, 1959.

Aristotle. *Aristotle's Poetics*. Trans. Leon Golden. Tallahassee: Florida State University Press, 1981.

———. *The Art of Rhetoric*. Trans. John Henry Freese. Loeb Classical Library 193. Cambridge, MA: Harvard University Press, 1967.

Berlin, Normand. *The Secret Cause: A Discussion of Tragedy.* Amherst: University of Massachusetts Press, 1981.

Benardete, Seth. *Sacred Transgressions: A Reading of Sophocles' "Antigone."* South Bend, IN: St. Augustine's Press, 1999.

Blundell, Mary Whitlock. *Helping Friends and Harming Enemies: A Study in Sophocles and Greek Ethics.* Cambridge: Cambridge University Press, 1989.

———, trans. *Antigone*. By Sophocles. Focus Classical Library. Newburyport, MA: Focus Information Group, 1998.

Boegehold, Alan L. *When a Gesture Was Expected*. Princeton, NJ: Princeton University Press, 1999.

Carpenter, Thomas H., and Christopher A. Faraone, eds. *Masks of Dionysus*. Ithaca, NY: Cornell University Press, 1993.

Cartledge, Paul. *Ancient Greek Political Thought in Practice.* Cambridge: Cambridge University Press, 2009.

Csapo, Eric. *Actors and Icons of the Ancient Theater.* West Sussex, UK: Wiley-Blackwell, 2000.

Csapo, Eric, and William J. Slater. *The Context of Ancient Drama.* Ann Arbor: University of Michigan Press, 1994.

Davidson, John N. *Courtesans and Fishcakes: The Consuming Passions of Classical Athens.* New York: St. Martin's Press, 1998.

Easterling, P. E., ed. *The Cambridge Companion to Greek Tragedy.* Cambridge: Cambridge University Press, 1997.

Edmunds, Lowell. *Theatrical Space and Historical Place in Sophocles' "Oedipus at Colonus."* Lanham, MD: Rowman & Littlefield, 1996.

Else, Gerald F. *The Origin and Early Form of Greek Tragedy.* New York: Norton, 1965.

Euripides. *Euripides.* The Complete Greek Tragedies, vol. 4. Ed. David Grene and Richmond Lattimore. Chicago: University of Chicago Press, 1959.

Foley, Helene P. *Female Acts in Greek Tragedy.* Princeton, NJ: Princeton University Press, 2001.

Garland, Robert. *The Greek Way of Death.* Ithaca, NY: Cornell University Press, 1985.

———. *The Greek Way of Life.* Ithaca, NY: Cornell University Press, 1990.

Goldhill, Simon. *Reading Greek Tragedy.* Cambridge: Cambridge University Press, 1986.

Goldhill, Simon, and Edith Hall. *Sophocles and the Greek Tragic Tradition.* Cambridge: Cambridge University Press, 2000.

Gould, Thomas. *The Ancient Quarrel Between Poetry and Philosophy*. Princeton, NJ: Princeton University Press, 1990.

———, trans. *"Oedipus the King": A Translation with Commentary*. By Sophocles. Englewood Cliffs, NJ: Prentice-Hall, 1970.

Grene, David, trans. *Sophocles 1*. 2nd ed. The Complete Greek Tragedies. Ed. David Grene and Richmond Lattimore. Chicago: University of Chicago Press, 1991.

Griffith, Mark, ed. *Antigone*. By Sophocles. Cambridge: Cambridge University Press, 1999.

Guthrie, W. K. C. *The Greeks and Their Gods*. Boston: Beacon Press, 1950.

Hanson, Victor Davis. *A War Like No Other*. New York: Random House, 2005.

Herodotus. *The Landmark Herodotus: The Histories*. Ed. Robert B. Strassler. New York: Pantheon Books, 2007.

Hughes, Bettany. *The Hemlock Cup: Socrates, Athens and the Search for the Good Life*. New York: Knopf, 2010.

Jebb, R. C., trans. *Antigone*. By Sophocles. Cambridge: Cambridge University Press, 1928. (Originally published 1888.)

Kagan, Donald. *Pericles of Athens and the Birth of Democracy*. New York: Touchstone–Simon & Schuster, 1991.

Kirkwood, G. M. *A Study of Sophoclean Drama*. Cornell Studies in Classical Philology 31. Ithaca, NY: Cornell University Press, 1994.

Knox, Bernard M. W. *Essays: Ancient and Modern*. Baltimore: Johns Hopkins University Press, 1989.

———. *The Heroic Temper: Studies in Sophoclean Tragedy*. Berkeley: University of California Press, 1964.

————. *Oedipus at Thebes*. New Haven, CT: Yale University Press, 1957.

————. Introduction and notes to *The Three Theban Plays*. By Sophocles. Trans. Robert Fagles. New York: Viking, 1982.

Lefkowitz, Mary R. *The Lives of Greek Poets*. Baltimore: Johns Hopkins University Press, 1981.

Lloyd-Jones, Hugh, trans. *Antigone*. By Sophocles. Loeb Classical Library 20. Cambridge, MA: Harvard University Press, 1994.

Lloyd-Jones, Hugh, and N. G. Wilson. *Hypomnemata*. Göttingen, Germany: Vandenhoeck & Ruprecht, 1997.

————. *Sophoclea: Studies on the Text of Sophocles*. Oxford: Clarendon Press, 1990.

Moore, J. A., trans. *Selections from the Greek Elegiac, Iambic, and Lyric Poets*. Cambridge, MA: Harvard University Press, 1947.

Pickard-Cambridge, Arthur. *The Dramatic Festivals of Athens*. 2nd ed. Revised with a new supplement by John Gould and D. M. Lewis. Oxford: Clarendon Press, 1988.

Plutarch. *The Rise and Fall of Athens: Nine Greek Lives*. Trans. Ian Scott-Kilvert. London: Penguin, 1960.

Radice, Betty. *Who's Who in the Ancient World*. London: Penguin, 1971.

Rehm, Rush. *The Play of Space: Spatial Transformation in Greek Tragedy*. Princeton, NJ: Princeton University Press, 2002.

Reinhardt, Karl. *Sophocles*. New York: Barnes & Noble– Harper & Row, 1979.

Seaford, Richard. *Reciprocity and Ritual: Homer and Tragedy in the Developing City-State*. Oxford: Clarendon Press, 1994.

Segal, Charles. *Antigone.* By Sophocles. Trans. Reginald Gibbons and Charles Segal. New York: Oxford University Press, 2003.

——. *Sophocles' Tragic World: Divinity, Nature, Society.* Cambridge, MA: Harvard University Press, 1995.

——. *Tragedy and Civilization: An Interpretation of Sophocles.* Cambridge, MA: Harvard University Press, 1981.

Steiner, George. *Antigones.* New Haven, CT: Yale University Press, 1996.

Taplin, Oliver. *Greek Tragedy in Action.* Berkeley: University of California Press, 1978.

Thucydides. *The Landmark Thucydides: A Comprehensive Guide to the Peloponnesian War.* Ed. Robert B. Strassler. New York: Touchstone–Simon & Schuster, 1996.

Tyrrell, Wm. Blake, and Larry J. Bennett. *Recapturing Sophocles' "Antigone."* Lanham, MD: Rowman & Littlefield, 1998.

Vernant, Jean-Pierre, ed. *The Greeks.* Trans. Charles Lambert and Teresa Lavender Fagan. Chicago: University of Chicago Press, 1995.

Vernant, Jean-Pierre, and Pierre Vidal-Naquet. *Myth and Tragedy in Ancient Greece.* Trans. Janet Lloyd. New York: Zone Books, 1990.

Whitman, C. E. *Sophocles.* Cambridge, MA: Harvard University Press, 1951.

Wiles, David. *Greek Theatre Performances: An Introduction.* Cambridge: Cambridge University Press, 2000.

——. *Tragedy in Athens: Performance Space and Theatrical Meaning.* Cambridge: Cambridge University Press, 1997.

Winkler, John J., and Froma I. Zeitlin, eds. *Nothing to Do with Dionysos?: Athenian Drama in Its Social Context*. Princeton, NJ: Princeton University Press, 1990.

Winnington-Ingram, R. P. *Sophocles: An Interpretation*. Cambridge: Cambridge University Press, 1980.

Zimmern, Alfred. *The Greek Commonwealth: Politics and Economics in Fifth-Century Greece*. 5th ed. New York: Modern Library, 1931.

ACKNOWLEDGMENTS

Translation is a thoroughly collaborative venture. The many scholars, theater practitioners, and friends who read and commented on this work at various stages deserve gratitude.

Three classicists, Thomas Fauss Gould, John Andrew Moore, and Charles Segal, did not live to see the publication of the present volume, but their influence and advice remains in the translations, introductions, and notes to the three Oedipus plays.

Mary Bagg's editing of the notes to this volume gave them clarity and accuracy they would not otherwise possess.

Thanks to the following readers for their contributions and suggestions: Normand Berlin, Michael Birtwistle, Alan L. Boegehold, Donald Junkins, Tracy Kidder, Robin Magowan, William Mullen, Arlene and James Scully, and Richard Trousdell.

Barbara Smith of the University of Utah Department of Theatre directed the first production of this translation of *Antigone* in September 2001; her production inspired revisions to the play as it is published here.

Special thanks to my agent, Wendy Strothman, who saw the possibility of a complete volume of Sophocles and skillfully helped accomplish it.

Robert Bagg is a graduate of Amherst College (1957). He received his PhD in English from the University of Connecticut (1965) and taught at the University of Washington (1963–65) and the University of Massachusetts, Amherst (1965–96), where he served as Graduate Director (1982–86) and Department Chair (1986–92). His awards include grants from the American Academy of Arts and Letters, the Ingram Merrill Foundation, the NEA and NEH, and the Guggenheim and Rockefeller foundations. His translations of Greek drama have been staged in sixty productions on three continents. Bagg, who is writing a critical biography of Richard Wilbur, lives in western Massachusetts with his wife, Mary Bagg, a freelance writer and editor.

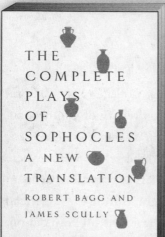
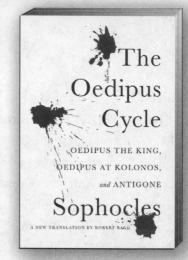